"While everyone is keenly aware of the imbalance between the number of male vs. female focused movies, few screenwriters have known where to turn to find help composing plots enthralling enough to tip the scales. The Archetype of the Virgin is a clever one to chose, as it evokes innocence on the one extreme, and solid self-possession on the other, an arc author Kim Hudson deftly delineates in *The Virgin's Promise*."
— Mary Trainor-Brigham, M.A., author of *Deep Cinema*

"A comprehensive answer to the age-old riddle of what do those feminine characters really want."
— John L. Geiger, co-author, *Creativity & Copyright*

"Far too many talented, hardworking women and minority screenwriters are underemployed compared to male screenwriters, and women's perspectives are far too often marginalized, trivialized or ignored in the film and television industries of our world. Kim Hudson's *The Virgin's Promise* will help both male and female screenwriters think about what's involved in creating more viable female characters, and provides a ready template for those who need one. I look forward to recommending this book to my screenwriting students."
— Alexis Krasilovsky, Professor, Dept. of Cinema and Television Arts, California State University, Northridge

"The story of the Virgin is as old as recorded history. Kim Hudson has given that story new life through her book. She has allowed readers to expand their imaginations to create a contemporary vision of this 'mythical' character. A must have for any writer's collection."
— Ken Rotcop, author of *The Perfect Pitch* and creator of Pitchmart

"Behind every great film is a great story of transformation. In *The Virgin's Promise*, Kim Hudson gives screenwriters a clear explanation of the archetypal journey toward feminine creative, spiritual, and sexual awakening. Highly recommended."
— Tony Levelle, author of *Digital Video Secrets* and co-author of *Producing with Passion*

"*The Virgin's Promise* finally delivers the inversion of the much-discussed Myth of the Hero. A long-overlooked female exploration of transformation, Hudson's analysis is revealing, engaging and informative. Screenwriters, scholars, and social studies grad students alike will be thanking her for years to come."
— Jay Miles, media instructor, East Haven (CT) High School

"Kim Hudson's new book, *The Virgin's Promise*, is both a powerful writing manual and a treasure of insight into the feminine nature. It will not only help you master the ability to write powerful female characters and develop the virgin's journey in fresh ways, but also help you see the deeper meaning in the stories of our lives. I admit I'm a sucker for this kind of stuff, but I believe Hudson has added a valuable volume that should be part of any writer's – or student of humanity's – library."

> – Derek Rydall, author of *I Could've Written a Better Movie than That!* and *There's No Business Like Soul Business*, founder, ScriptwriterCentral.com, EnlightenedEntertainer.com.

"*The Virgin's Promise* is a groundbreaking and profound addition to the canon on screenplay structure. With great clarity Kim Hudson offers a method for understanding and writing successful screenplays about characters whose dramatic journey follows an internal path to discovery and acceptance of their true identity in spite of formidable obstacles. I am certain that many important and successful new films will be inspired by this book."

> – Sharon McGowan, producer of *Better Than Chocolate* and *The Lotus Eaters*

"A story well told can change the world. Hudson unlocks the secret to writing stories of self-fulfillment in this lovely and inspiring book. A must read for all storytellers and screenwriters."

> – Mireille Soria, producer of *Ever After*

"For a work as thought provoking and even profound as this, *The Virgin's Promise* is thankfully accessible and not for a minute esoteric during its read. The icing on the cake is Hudson's style and use of language. At once simple and yet complex. *The Virgin's Promise* is a bit like the perfect haiku: Sparse and philosophical."

> – Deepa Mehta, screenwriter/producer of *Fire, Earth, Water* and *Bollywood/Hollywood*

PROMISE

WRITING STORIES OF FEMININE CREATIVE, SPIRITUAL, AND SEXUAL AWAKENING

KIM HUDSON

MICHAEL WIESE PRODUCTIONS

Published by Michael Wiese Productions
12400 Ventura Blvd. #1111
Studio City, CA 91604
(818) 379-8799, (818) 986-3408 (FAX)
mw@mwp.com
www.mwp.com

Cover design by MWP
Interior design by William Morosi
Edited by Paul Norlen
Printed by McNaughton & Gunn

Manufactured in the United States of America

Library of Congress Cataloging-in-Publication Data

Hudson, Kim, 1960-
 The virgin's promise : writing stories of feminine creative, spiritual, and sexual awakening / Kim Hudson.
    p. cm. -- (Great unproduced film scripts)
 Includes bibliographical references.
 ISBN 978-1-932907-72-8
1. Motion picture authorship. 2. Motion picture plays--Technique. 3. Archetype (Psychology) 4. Archetype (Psychology) in motion pictures. 5. Characters and characteristics in motion pictures. 6. Virgins. 7. Femininity. I. Title.
PN1996.H74 2010
808.2'3082--dc22

                          2009053119

Printed on Recycled Stock

To Jamie, Jesse and Buzz

Contents

List of Tables

Acknowledgements

riting *The Virgin's Promise* has been a five-year journey of exploration for me. I kept pursuing this path thanks to people who encouraged me when the idea was young and fragile. People like Clodagh O'Connell, Harvey McKinnon, Harold Johnson, Lori Hudson-Fish, and many others I encountered along the way. The generous support of Dave Joe gave me the space to explore these ideas and write while still caring for our children in a soulful way, which was a real gift. I am grateful to Michael Wiese Productions for taking a chance on a first-time author with a dream. A sincere thank you also to my editors Silvia Heinrich, Melva McLean and Pat Sanders; my readers Gervais Bushe, Joyce Thierry, Mark Timko, Kent Robertson, Laurie Anderson, Robyn Harding, and Colleen Jones; and my friends Luke Carroll, Katherine and Rob Strother, George Maddison, Marcia Thomson, Laurel Parry, and Louise Hardy who were so generous with their time and insights. And finally, thank you to my daughters Jesse and Jamie who have enormous faith in me, and to Laurie Anderson who is a true hero to me.

Foreword

by Christopher Vogler

he "Hero's Journey" pattern that Joseph Campbell wrote about in *The Hero with a Thousand Faces* has been a wellspring of creativity and inspiration for many people, male and female, who recognized the patterns as a metaphorical description of their journeys through life. It has been a roadmap for storytellers and artists, female and male, who find its terms and incidents to be perfectly designed to connect with the emotions and dreams of their audiences. For many people it can be a universal, one-size-fits-all guidebook to the inevitable stages of life, travel, launching a new business, or any serious endeavor.

However, and this is a big however, there has been a persistent shortcoming in this approach to life and literature, in that it has a slight gender bias towards the masculine. In my work I try to view it as neutral, genderless, a description of the general human condition, but it has been pointed out to me many times, and I have come to understand on my own, that there is more than a drop of testosterone in the assumptions and specifics of the Hero's Journey, starting with that word "hero." I noticed that when I started lecturing about the Hero's Journey, many people immediately assumed I was talking about male action heroes, superheroes, traditionally male military heroes, etc. Women would say "Fine, I get it about the man's journey to go out and conquer something, but what's the woman's journey?"

I had no good answer. I am a man, I see things as a man, and it would be foolish to speculate what it's like to be a woman on her journey through life. So I looked around and found the work of female scholars like Marie-Louise von Franz, Marija Gimbutas, Maureen Murdock, and Carol Pearson on the mythic archetypes specific to women, and the very different ways they saw the journey. Kim Hudson, the author of the book in your hands, doesn't even think of it as necessarily being a journey, but rather an emotional process. Maureen Murdock in particular had a way of restating the unique life patterns and signposts of the woman's experience as a clear outline, so I began referring people who wondered "What is the Woman's Journey?" to Murdock's work.

But I felt there was more work to be done in this area, especially in applying the findings of sociologists, scholars, and therapists to the specialized worlds of storytelling and screenwriting, and I encouraged my questioners and all the women in the audience to develop a theory about what is unique about the feminine experience of drama and life's patterns.

I was encouraged all along by the enthusiasm with which women, especially my friends in the world of romance novel writing, took to the Hero's Journey as a useful template or toolbox for designing and troubleshooting their works. They could definitely see themselves reflected in it, but at the same time they felt free to amend it and rephrase it so it made sense from the feminine perspective. They emphasized some elements and diminished others as they saw fit, and changed terminology to reflect the realities of their business, the desires of their audiences, and the guidance of their own hearts. That seems in keeping with Joseph Campbell's idea that the Hero has a thousand faces, countless interpretations, "the one, shape-shifting yet marvelously constant story that we find, together with a challengingly persistent suggestion of more remaining to be experienced than will ever be known or told" (Campbell, *The Hero with a Thousand Faces*). And among the shifting shapes must surely be plenty of uniquely female expressions.

I have a few guesses about the differences between the masculine and feminine approaches to dramatic structure, and one of them focuses on geometry. What geometric form makes a somewhat accurate model of how you see drama unfolding? Stories can be represented graphically by a straight line like a railroad track, as Syd Field diagrams screenplays in his books. You use a pyramid or a ballistic curve to represent the arc of the story, or as Campbell chose, and I have chosen to follow, you can trace the stages of a story as a circle. When women describe to me how they experience drama or a dramatic event in their lives, the graphic patterns that come to mind are a series of concentric circles or a spiral in which the female protagonist proceeds more inwardly through a series of levels than the male who tends to move out into the world. The female heroes seem to move towards the center of a series of rings that represent the different levels of female relationships – relationship with father and mother, other women, men, children, society, the gods and goddesses, and finally at the center with themselves, their own true natures. Then they may return through all those levels, unwinding the spiral, applying what they have learned at their center to each set of relationships. They may touch upon some or all of the stages of the Hero's Journey while they trace their own geometry, but they seem to be more interested in these relationships than in the external adventures and physical challenges.

But I have been hoping someone would take on this subject with full commitment to work out the details of a comprehensive theory of drama from a feminine perspective, and I believe you are about to read a book that does exactly that.

What I found in these pages was an eye-opening re-telling of the universal human story from the feminine perspective, with quite different language and thinking than I had ever considered. Hudson starts by overthrowing the troublesome words hero and heroine and strikes out boldly to trace the unique adventure of the Virgin archetype. Many of the terms she uses are compatible with those of the Hero's Journey, and simply emphasize a different shade of meaning in some common signposts. But other elements of her grammar of storytelling are unique, recognizing turning points that don't have equivalents in the Hero's Journey language, that are uniquely feminine, or at least reflective of a more inward and emotionally based approach to drama and life. She leaves plenty of room for male heroes to experience their own version of the Virgin's Promise, suggesting the term "Prince" as the male counterpart of Virgin.

I have known a few Hollywood princelings in my career, sons and grandsons of powerful people who stood to inherit kingdoms, and so I heartily endorse the exploration of this rich archetype, which Shakespeare pioneered with his studies of the playboy prince Hal turning into the stalwart King Henry V.

Among the many revelations in this book is the author's technique of pairing archetypes, which yields many useful diagrams and insights. For example, she pairs the Virgin with its polar opposite, the Whore, and shows how the two archetypes intertwine and reflect each other. Another useful pairing is the Hero and the Coward, with Coward replacing the terms I typically use to describe the hero's moral opposite, Villain and Shadow. The choice of Coward emphasizes the unspoken quality of courage in the term Hero, and points out a deep and consistent truth about Villains and Shadow figures – they are cowards, choosing a selfish and greedy path rather than the heroic path of self-sacrifice for the greater good.

This book repeatedly pounds me with how much I didn't know. The author has done a thorough, and I mean thorough, research job on archetypes and psychological theory, and you won't find a more lucid guide to these sometimes challenging concepts. I have already mentioned Hudson's useful diagrams that show the variations of the male and female archetypes and their positive and negative potentials at different stages of life; these alone are worth the price of the book. But there are many more nuggets of value in here, including a groundbreaking distinction between fairy tales and myths. The author maintains that fairy tales are generally the province of the feminine and tend to be domestic and family-oriented, and that myths for the most part are the outer-directed territory of masculine energy. She is not dogmatic on this or any other point, and gives ample acknowledgement of the exceptions.

Having identified them as the key to understanding the Virgin's Promise concept, Kim Hudson caresses the fairy tales to bring out every nuance of their meaning for the storyteller who wants to accurately express the feminine experience.

The author has taken care to draw parallels and make correspondences with both Campbell's language and mine, so that the Hero's Journey is not rejected but acknowledged as part of a larger system that also includes the Virgin's Promise. The two approaches are seen as complementary rather than confrontational, and combining the two of them will give you a complete set of language and mental tools for dealing with any kind of story.

I have always said that the screenwriter or novelist needs a lot of tools and a lot of language to manage and describe the many possibilities in these crafts. No one set of terms can encompass all the human possibilities, and so we need many templates, many models, many sets of terms to describe them to ourselves and communicate them to other artists. This book makes a substantial contribution to the lingo and the tools and will stimulate further thinking about this subject. For example, I have always felt that the Hero's Journey is actually asexual and genderless, and therefore someone needs to do for the uniquely masculine journey what Kim Hudson has done for the feminine.

Until then, here is a work that fills a major gap in the theory of drama and life. One more thing before this foreword becomes longer than the book it introduces. I am struck by the persistence of light in this vision of the feminine experience. Light seems to be a uniting metaphor in this framework. Three of Hudson's thirteen stages, "Opportunity to Shine." "Caught Shining," and "Chooses her Light" directly mention aspects of light and there are glimmers of light throughout the theory. Hudson reminds us that "Just as the Greek goddess Aphrodite was known for her radiance, the shining forth of an internal quality rather than any physical attribute, the Virgin's beauty is often described in terms of light such as shining, glowing, brilliant, dazzling and iridescent... In other words, the Virgin's beauty represents the shining forth of her soul." In that spirit, this book brings light to the mysteries of the unique feminine experience of life's journey, and delivers a boon to screenwriters and storytellers of all kinds.

Christopher Vogler

Preface

*a*s I developed this theory of the Virgin archetypal journey, it dawned on me that my life was following the Virgin story. I was a wife in a privileged life, busy caring for my family, and pushing my fascination with story aside. One day I noticed an ad for a Writing for Film and Television program. I thought that perhaps writing screenplays might be the easiest way to start. It's all dialogue. How hard could that be? I had a lot to learn but the thought gave me permission to do it.

On the first day of school I was all nerves, but I had a plan for survival. I would blend in with the crowd. Lay low and learn was my motto. Getting here had been a work of progressive requests and assurances until finally the space was carved out for a few months – secretly I hoped it would be for a lifetime. I decided to wear faded blue jeans and a white poet's blouse, hoping to give a youthful, artsy impression. From a distance no one would suspect I was over forty. My God, my classmates were young-faced! A woman welcomed us and read a poem by Marion Williamson. By the time she got to "We ask ourselves, 'Who am I to be brilliant, gorgeous, talented and famous?'," I was sure she was talking directly to me.

Randomly, people were asked to introduce themselves. I slouched, made no eye contact, and silently chanted "lay low and learn," but the instructor stood in front of me and asked me to speak. It was a classic opportunity to shine in the Virgin archetypal story.

I stood up and blurted out, "I had my fortieth birthday and suddenly realized if I don't try something now, this will be all that there is." I slipped back into my chair, pretty sure I'd blown any effect my poet blouse was giving.

Eventually, a psychologist joined us. He spoke on the works of mythologist Joseph Campbell, psychiatrist Carl Jung, Hollywood story editor Christopher Vogler, and the story of the Hero's Journey. I was in love. And I don't say this lightly. The concepts just jumped out at me as truths. He described inherited archetypes that connect all humans through time. An archetype represented each of the three stages of the masculine and feminine life: beginning, middle, and end. Each stage had an accompanying shadow side, making a total of twelve archetypes. We, the three hundred people in the theater, were going to brainstorm and pull these archetypes from our collective unconscious pool.

We began by questing for a name for the beginning stage masculine archetype. Hero was chorused by the crowd. The shadow side, Coward, didn't cause the crowd to stall, either. The masculine at the height of his power was described as Father/King/God, which I vaguely remembered from an art class. We struggled to name the shadow side of being a mature masculine archetype and were rewarded with the Tyrant. Very satisfying! Then we found words for the elderly masculine archetype including Mentor, Wise Man, and Merlin. His shadow side, a Lecher, made me chuckle.

We turned to the feminine side and stalled. The psychologist wrote "Princess/Virgin" to describe the beginning feminine archetype. I was intrigued by the association of sexuality with a feminine archetype. The description of the shadow side of the beginning feminine archetype was the Whore. Yikes!

People enthusiastically shouted out mature feminine archetype names like Mother, Queen, and Goddess. The call for the shadow side left the room popping with suggestions: Evil Stepmother, Wicked Queen. This seemed plainly wrong. That wasn't a shadow side – that was the same as the light side, except not very nice about it. The more I thought about it, Queen was more the female version of King than an opposite. I adjusted the mature feminine to Mother/Goddess in my mind. While I was at it, I decided that the masculine in my version is Lover/King. I smiled at myself. Only three hours into it and I was already questioning great thinkers like Campbell and Vogler. Then I thought that maybe this is the point. Every one of us has the ability to reach inside ourselves, look for a feeling of resonance, and make a connection with the archetypes in our own way.

The instructor called for an example of a positive image for the end stage feminine archetype. The auditorium was silent, making me feel entirely justified in my earlier vanity. Slowly I raised my hand.

"Crone?"

Several people argued that Crone was a negative archetype, but eventually it was determined she may create unpleasant circumstances, but they benefit others, so she was a light side archetype. Crone, Wise Woman, and Fairy Godmother were added to our archetypal list. For the description of the shadow side of an end stage feminine archetype, "Witch" was eagerly shouted out and accepted. I was uncomfortable writing this down. A witch may not see herself as operating from the shadow side. I was sure archetypes had to be unbiased and universal.

We paused and looked at our chart. There it was, brought up from its storage place in our collective unconscious. Then I heard that the Hero archetype also had a repeated progression of actions that mapped out a full, meaningful experience. The

Hero lives in an **Ordinary World** until one day he receives a **Call to Adventure**. At first he **Refuses the Call**, because of the great danger, but after **Meeting with the Guide**, the Hero **Crosses the First Threshold** to a foreign land. Suddenly away from everything familiar, the Hero is tested in his ability to survive. Clear in his purpose he meets allies who can help him and learns about his enemy. The allies make **Preparations** to enter the enemy's lair and increase their chances of success. The Hero faces near-death in a **Crisis**, escapes with his life, and is **Rewarded** with an advantage when next he faces the enemy. He takes the **Road Back** and meets the enemy in a **Final Battle**. The Hero defeats the enemy, sometimes at the cost of his life, and **Returns with the Elixir** that will keep the village safe.

We were told that in Campbell's theory, all story, throughout history and across all cultures, follows a mono-myth which he called the Hero's Journey; the story of the beginning stage masculine archetype, which applies equally to women and men.

Lay low and learn. I couldn't do it. "What about the whole other side of the chart?" I inquired, nodding to the feminine archetypes.

"Well," the psychologist answered, "the feminine archetypes are considered more passive and internal. Good in novels, but movies are all about action."

This did not sit right with me. For weeks, concepts of archetypes kept churning in my head as I kept doing my double shifts, film-school student by day, mom by night. Suddenly I found myself inexplicably weeping on the bus, in my instructor's office, alone at home. One day my instructor said, "It is amazing how hard people work to stay stuck." He was talking about my screenplay character but that was exactly what I was doing. I needed to stop hiding in my marriage and make room for this research.

Back and forth on the bus I kept wrestling with the concept that the Virgin archetype also had a pattern of behavior. Repeated beats emerged from watching many non-hero movies.

The Virgin begins her story in a **Dependent World**. She carries her kingdom's hopes for their continuation, which are contrary to her dream for herself. At first she is afraid to go against her community and realize her own dream. But then she has a small **Opportunity** to follow her dream in secret. She acknowledges her dream by **Dressing the Part**, if only temporarily. Enlivened by this first experience, the Virgin goes back and forth, juggling the two worlds, enhancing her dream in the **Secret World**, while appeasing her **Dependent World**. Eventually she **No Longer Fits Her World** and she gets **Caught Shining**. In this crisis the Virgin has a moment of clarity and **Gives Up What Has Been Keeping Her Stuck**. The **Kingdom Goes into Chaos**. Now, she **Wanders in the Wilderness** trying to decide whether she will make herself small again to make people happy or choose to live her dream. She **Chooses Her Light**! She loses her protection and it is grim, but the kingdom **Re-orders** itself to accommodate the blossoming Virgin, and changes for the better.

I decided to get unstuck and believe in myself. I studied myths, legends, scriptures, and theories of mythology and anthropology. I attended lectures at the Jungian Institute in Switzerland and read the leading books on screenwriting theory, Jungian archetypal theory, and myths and fairy tales. I analyzed movies chosen for their Virgin theme as well as their popularity.

Despite child-raising commitments, caring for my mother, and the inevitable end of my marriage, I kept rewriting, editing, and sharing my theory. I believed in the world of archetypes and in return the archetypes inspired me, educated me, and gave me a passion for life.

Archetypes are a very rich and fascinating area. They touch what is universal and meaningful in us. In your hands you have the bones for writing stories that awaken our feminine potential through creative, spiritual and sexual being. This is only the beginning. My greatest dream is that it will inspire your creative energy and lead to rewarding storytelling experiences.

Introduction

he Virgin's promise encompasses both the obligations and expectations from her community, and her personal potential that longs to be fulfilled. The Virgin is pulled apart by these forces as she quests to know herself and be herself. *The Virgin's Promise: Writing Feminine Stories of Creative, Spiritual, and Sexual Awakening* challenges the assumption that every story is centered on a hero, and proposes that the Virgin has a unique archetypal path. It does this by describing the Virgin structure and showing how the two structures are separate yet work in support of one other. This book is for writers and movie buffs who want to expand their understanding of stories with the addition of a feminine archetypal structure.

Theorist and storyteller Joseph Campbell opens his book *The Hero with a Thousand Faces* with a chapter on the mono-myth. He states:

> Whether we listen with aloof amusement to the dream like mumbo jumbo of some red-eyed witch doctor of the Congo, or read with cultivated rapture thin translations from the sonnets of the mystic Lao-tse;... [the Hero's Journey] will be always the one, shape-shifting yet marvelously constant story that we find... (3)

But a second model exists: the Virgin's Promise, which balances the masculine with its feminine counterpoint, as in yin and yang. This book explores the archetypal journey of coming into being. These may be stand-alone Virgin movies as in *Ever After*; stories where the protagonist grows on both the Virgin and Hero levels simultaneously, as in *Mulan*; or movies with a fully developed Virgin story alongside a fully developed Hero story, as seen in *Shrek*.

I began my exploration of the Virgin archetype noticing those elements in movies, myths, and fairy tales that contribute to the theme of being true to yourself. I compared these repeated elements with Jungian theory on the Virgin archetype, which described her as developing the art of Becoming and Being, and found they were remarkably consistent. The result is *The Virgin's Promise*, made up of thirteen repeated steps or beats.

The word "beats" can be confusing because it is also used in screenwriting literature to describe pacing elements similar to scene breakdowns with an action and a reaction, and also a momentary pause in the dialogue. Here, the term "beat" is strictly used to describe plot points, which are the key events, decisions, or discoveries made by the Virgin, or Hero, that move the protagonist along on her/his journey.

In this theory, there is an important distinction made between feminine and female. While an archetype may embody a feminine energy, it is not necessarily female. Archetypes are applicable to both genders equally. To make this point, I have used examples of male and female Virgins when I describe the Virgin structure and, likewise, female and male Heroes to demonstrate the Hero structure. I have, however, defaulted to the pronouns "she" for the Virgin and "he" for the Hero to avoid the awkwardness of excessive use of s/he.

Coupling maleness with femininity may feel strange, especially when the Virgin isn't necessarily gay. Prince can be substituted in your mind for Virgin if it seems more appropriate for a male character, since the Prince too represents a character born to a set of expectations that limit his ability to realize his personal vision for his life. Think of Scott in *Strictly Ballroom*, Rocky in *Rocky* or John in *Wedding Crashers*. They are all Virgins by my definition, dreaming of achieving their inner potential. That's not to say realization of your authentic sexual orientation doesn't make a great Virgin story. It does, as shown by Ennis in *Brokeback Mountain*, Maggie in *Better Than Chocolate*, and Martha in *The Children's Hour*.

The bringing of the Virgin's dream for herself into the physical world often occurs through the development of the inherently feminine aspects of creativity, sexuality, and spirituality (Murdock, 5). Creative awakening is like an act of alchemy. The artist looks inside and finds a way to express a piece of herself. We all recognize this shining element of self being brought forward when we see an inspiring dancer, are moved by a great pianist or rock band, or view an evocative painting. A person's essence is communicated and shared by turning it into an art form.

Similarly, sexual awakening is a form of allowing an internal sense of self to flower into physical acts. The recognition of a personal desire that is claimed as one's own and acted on is a profound act of acquiring personal authority. Coming of Age movies depict the first sexual experience, a metaphor for becoming an independent person by bringing an inner desire to life.

The spiritual awakening of the Virgin is the art of being. It is a multilayered concept that means different things to different people. It may be found in the claiming of one's goodness. Its enemy is envy which attacks the existence of another and is spiritually deadening. The Virgin archetype heals this effect by guiding the way towards embracing who she knows herself to be. The Virgin may also embody the belief that there is a piece of the divine in all of us such as a dream or a talent which is brought out by the actions of the Virgin. This is expressed when a person has a calling or a natural gift. The expression of spirituality also occurs when a person believes in something greater than themselves such as the Muses, God, or love. Sports movies are examples of spiritual quests where the small town team goes for the cup against all odds. Wish-fulfillment movies also show a belief in something outside of oneself.

The story of the Virgin or Princess has been with us as long as stories have been told (Zipes, 17). However, until now a cohesive theory as to the archetypal structure of the Virgin has not been formulated as it has for the Hero (see Campbell and Vogler). As a result, the Virgin is often reduced to the role she plays within the Hero story. The need for an understanding of the Virgin becomes profound when it is recognized that archetypal stories are roadmaps for life (Stevens, 1999, 38). We need to be more than brave, self-sacrificing Heroes. We also need to be Virgins who bring our inner talents and self-fulfilling joys to life. And we need stories that show us how to do that.

This book is structured in two parts. Part One introduces basics of Jungian theory as a foundation for understanding the archetypes. It also explores the symbolic nature of the twelve key archetypes: the Virgin, Hero, Whore, Coward, Mother/Goddess, Lover/King, Femme Fatale, Tyrant, Crone, Mentor, Hag and Miser. It then looks closely at the Virgin and the Hero structures to give clarity to each beat. Examples from a range of movies are used to illustrate various aspects of these structures. Film summaries are provided to highlight the archetypal beats of some of these movies. The summaries are also useful if the movie example is unfamiliar.

An exploration of the Hero structure is included here because the Virgin and the Hero are, in many ways, polar opposites of each other. Understanding one gives a greater understanding of the other, just as white looks sharpest against black. In this way, the Hero structure contributes to an understanding of the Virgin structure. The Virgin structure also focuses the Hero structure.

Including the Hero archetype provides a comparative framework for understanding the Virgin and makes it easy to reference the points being made on how the two journeys cross over, support each other, and are distinct.

Part Two of this book opens with a summary of screenwriting structural theory. These sections provide the background within which writers generally work and an introduction to how the Virgin structure fits into existing theory. Screenwriters are then guided through the application of this archetypal theory with a beat-sheet for structuring a screenplay and a discussion on using the beats to identify the story's central question, create a log line and strengthen the internal connections in the story.

The Virgin's Promise provides a pathway into the feminine archetypal journey lying dormant in our collective unconscious. The quest to become true to yourself. This theory offers a new way to view movies, and gives writers of all kinds, and particularly screenwriters, the resources to invoke this feminine archetypal magic.

Part I

Chapter 1

Archetypal Theory

ne of my favorite moments in the movie *Ever After* occurs when Danielle, a Cinderella character, says to her wicked stepmother, "Do it yourself." It's one of those great "aha" moments. Despite the fact that I know this line is coming and I've seen it at least a dozen times, I look forward to this scene every time. It has all the features of being in touch with an archetype: the audience is willing to see it repeatedly; they instinctively recognize the situation and feel elated with the action taken; and they easily remember that moment after it's over.

Psychiatrist Carl Jung explored the concept of archetypes and proposed that there is a consistent set of archetypes in every human. He suggested our collective unconscious causes us to be drawn to these images and behaviors because they give us a sense of direction, meaning in life, and a feeling of euphoria (Stein, 100). This is the reason we look to archetypal structure when we write.

Basics of Jungian Theory

Carl Jung set out to map the *terra incognita* of the human soul. Over his lifetime he developed his theory of archetypes. On one level, the theory is complicated, attempting to explain the ego and the soul, and many abstract thoughts in between. On another level, the theory refers to aspects of ourselves as humans and is therefore very familiar.

Jung proposed that we have three psychic levels: the conscious, the personal unconscious, and the collective unconscious. The conscious houses our memory and understanding of the events of our daily life. The personal unconscious contains those life experiences and memories that are repressed or not understood. They are acquired through life experience and therefore are not common to everyone (Jung, 1976, 38). The third psychic level, the collective unconscious, is inherited and common to all people, now and throughout history. This is where the archetypes reside.

The theories of psychoanalysts Sigmund Freud and Alfred Adler deal mainly with the second psychic level, the personal unconscious. These theories are working with complexes, which develop as a result of a personal trauma. A complex is a pattern of behavior or a belief designed to protect oneself from repeating actions that previously caused pain. They work on a level of which we are not consciously aware. For example, Freud is said to have had a repressed history of sexual entanglement with his sister-in-law, which resulted in his seeing most issues through a sexual lens (Jung, 1976, xvi). Adler experienced strong sibling rivalry which caused him to focus on interpersonal power dynamics and resulted in his theory of the urge for self-assertion, the drive to get the most you can for yourself (Jung, 1976, xv, 61).

Problems often arise when the complex, designed when resources were limited, keeps operating in an adult. Sometimes the complex grows and adapts itself to new situations. The Joker in *Dark Knight* is a strong example of a character driven by an unconscious complex created by an earlier life experience. The Joker is constantly asserting that all humans are self-focused and self-preserving to the detriment of others. He unconsciously developed this belief, possibly to explain the abuse he suffered at the hands of his father. Rather than believe his father did not love him, he sets out to prove all humans are predisposed to sadistic behavior.

The complexes of Freud and Adler differ from Jung's theory of archetypes in two major ways. First, complexes are based on events that originated in the conscious and were pushed to the personal unconscious. They are dependent on the personal history of an individual for their development. In contrast, we are born with archetypes and their patterns of behavior.

Second, Jung believed the human psyche has a mechanism to look backward after a crisis, and a mechanism to look forward when facing a challenge. Complexes are meant to stop physical and psychological movement into the unknown. Archetypes are "patterns of instinctual behavior" (Jung, 1976, 61) humans can invoke to gain insights into how to move ahead. Through dreams, myths, and fairy tales, with their inherent archetypal patterns, we are pointed towards "a higher potential health, not simply backward to past crises" (Jung, 1976, xxii). In many ways these two mechanisms keep us balanced between safety and risk. Complexes create protective barriers and archetypes act as guides towards greater human potentials.

Jung described archetypes as both a source of psychic symbols and a predisposition to react, behave and interact in a certain way (in movie terms they are analogous to both a character and a character arc). These two aspects make archetypes very powerful. He felt they carry the energy that ultimately creates civilization and culture (Stein, 4, 85).

Archetypes have a light and a shadow side, both of which are important for going through transformations. Light side archetypes such as the Virgin and Hero represent the higher human potential. Shadow characters, for example the Whore and the Coward, represent the counterpart, which either becomes the starting point for growth, the inspiration for growth or a point of reference.

The shadow side archetype may represent the immature, stunted aspect of each stage of life (Moore, xvii) and has several functions in storytelling. It may be the position from which the protagonist will grow. The Virgin has a moment as the Whore who sells her dream to appease others. The Hero starts out as the Coward, refusing to go on the adventure. The shadow may also represent the consequence of not going through the archetypal journey, as in a cautionary tale. More often, shadow side characters, or archetypes, make great antagonists whose function is to propel the protagonist forward on his/her journey.

The shadow side archetype is inherently the opposite of its light side archetype. Viewing them as a pair of opposites highlights the important aspects of each archetype. You see more clearly what it is by looking at what it is not. The shadow defines the light. For example, the Virgin moves towards joy to realize her dream. The Whore feels victimized and loses her autonomy to the control of others and their fantasies. The Virgin is a valued commodity and the Whore is scorned by society. The fundamental differences between these two characters add clarity to each of them. The Hero looks braver when the Coward beside him has five good reasons to run away.

Jung felt that the function of story was to guide us through the universal transformations of life, collectively known as individuation, using archetypes with their symbolic characters and patterns of behavior. The first risk of life is to stand on your own, and take up your individual power. This is the challenge of developing a relationship with yourself and the work of the Virgin and the Hero. The next challenge is to learn to use your power well and join in a partnership with another person, as the Lover/King and Mother/Goddess must do. The final challenge is to join the cosmos, to focus on giving back and letting go and seeing the beauty of one's insignificance. This task is guided by the Crone and the Mentor. You can refuse to take up these tasks but nobody gets off the planet without facing these challenges. Audiences find meaning in and are entertained by this quest for individuation.

Fairy Tales and Myths

Jung theorized the existence of archetypes after observing that myths and fairy tales of world literature have repeated beats or motifs (Jung, 1965, 392). In *Orality and Literacy,* philosopher Walter Ong describes how in oral cultures, where the story is memorized, non-essential information is dropped with each retelling, and the core patterns emerge strongly (Ong, 59, 60). The same effect is created in movies, which are delivered in roughly an hour and a half. In order to meet this restriction, the clutter is removed, and the archetypal beats become vivid.

Generally, Virgin stories occur in the realm of fairy tales and Hero stories occur in the realm of mythology. There are exceptions, such as the Virgin themed side-story of *Cupid and Psyche* found in the Roman writer Lucius Apuleius's myth, the *Golden Ass.* However, it is interesting to consider why the Princess/Virgin plays a leading role in many fairy tales while myths often center on the Hero. Possibly this difference is rooted in the internal versus external nature of the Virgin and the Hero journeys, respectively.

In Bruno Bettelheim's book *The Uses of Enchantment: The Meaning and Importance of Fairy Tales,* he notes that fairy tales are centered on self-worth and selfhood (1989, 6, 7, 24). This is a natural device for the Virgin who seeks to bring her authentic self to life by following her dreams. The Virgin must answer the question: Who do I know myself to be and what do I want to do in the world, separate from what everyone else wants of me?

Fairy tales are presented as stories of casual, everyday life events, which take place in the domestic realm (Bettelheim, 37). The Virgin confronts her central question in her childhood environment with its teachings and expectations because these are the forces that compete in her mind as she seeks to define herself as an individual. Her journey is towards psychological independence.

Myths are centered on themes of place in the world of obligation. This is the realm of the Hero as he seeks to answer the question, "Could I survive in the greater world or am I to forever cling to the nurturing world of my mother for fear of death?" His journey is towards physical independence.

Myth presents a world or circumstance that is absolutely unique (Bettelheim, 37). This is compatible with the Hero's journey to a foreign land. Surrounded by the unfamiliar, the Hero faces the challenge of learning the physical boundaries within which he can survive.

When the Hero explores his boundaries he is pushing the edges of mortality. He is tampering with the boundaries between mortals and gods, because immortality is a right of the gods. Heroes, therefore, find themselves battling with villains who seem immortal in stories of grand proportions. The Hero is often unknowingly of half-immortal parentage, a metaphor for questing for the boundaries of his mortality. These features associate Hero stories with myths.

Another feature distinguishing fairy tales and myths is that the characters in fairy tales are generic and common (Bettelheim, 1989, 40). They are father, mother, a princess, king or prince. Only the main figure has a name and often not in the title. It is *Beauty and the Beast,* any beauty and any beast. *The Goose Girl* and *The Ugly Duckling* both use general descriptions rather than names. Characters in myths, on the other hand, are very specific (Bettelheim, 40). It is the myth of Theseus and the Minotaur, rather than the general story of a hero and a beast. This again speaks to the general and casual atmosphere of fairy tales and the portrayal of a unique circumstance in myths.

Both fairy tales and myths acknowledge the difficulties of life and offer solutions. The fairy tale has a happy and optimistic style with the assurance of a resolution and a happily-ever-after ending. Our enjoyment of a fairy tale induces us to respond to the message of the story. As with the Virgin, it is a pull towards joy that drives her transformation. The Hero is driven by the need to conquer fear. The myth is more often a tragic tale of hardship with an overall pessimism (Bettelheim, 37, 43).

The happily-ever-after ending of fairy tales (Zipes, 9) also speaks to the spiritual nature of the Virgin story. Magic and optimism are metaphors for the belief that something greater than ourselves is at work for us. The pessimism of myths connects with the Hero's need to face hardship and the fact of death and deal with the fear in a physical way.

James Hollis, a Jungian theorist, describes the study of myth as an avenue to understanding the meaning in life. The stuff of myths is "that which connects us most deeply with our own nature and our place in the cosmos" (Hollis, 2004, 8). With the introduction of the Virgin archetypal structure, I would argue that the same is true for the study of fairy tales.

Archetypal Themes

In addition to being symbolic characters, archetypes model pathways for the universal transformations in life. The work of Joseph Campbell, later customized for the movie industry by Christopher Vogler in his book *The Writer's Journey* (1998), captures the twelve beats of the Hero's Journey. In a similar way, this book offers a new theory that lays out thirteen beats common to the Virgin Story.

Comprehensive analyses of the beats for the other core archetypes are not yet available but I believe that if there are two archetypal journeys, there are more. The following description of the essential nature of the Virgin, Whore, Hero, Coward, Lover/King, Tyrant, Mother/Goddess, Femme Fatale, Mentor, Miser, Crone and Hag may provide the groundwork for that future analysis. A basic understanding of these archetypes is also useful for creating strong characters.

These archetypes represent the three stages or acts of life: beginning, middle and end; child, adult, and elder. A movie generally follows a protagonist through one of the stages showing the arc of that transformation. It may also be peopled with characters at various different stages, all interacting with each other's journeys. A character may represent a different archetype for some parts of the movie, but a dominant thread for one archetypal transformation is generally woven through the movie.

The Virgin, the Whore, the Hero and the Coward all represent the beginning stage of the three acts of life. Born into a dependent situation, every human must know who they are as an individual before they can reach their potential. Therefore, these four archetypes are concerned with the relationship a person has with oneself. It is the time for learning to stand on your own and take up your power.

The Virgin takes on the task of claiming her personal authority, even against the wishes of others. A big part of her story therefore is how she is viewed by society. Initially she is a valued commodity for being pure, untouched, good, kind, nice, compliant, agreeable, or helpful. She carries the hope for continuation of the virtues of a society. Through her journey she learns to redefine her values and bring her true self into being. She is well represented in movies like *Bend It Like Beckham*, *Billy Elliot*, and *Shakespeare in Love*.

The Hero takes on the task of expanding his boundaries in the world, at the risk of death. Driven by a desire to help his community, the Hero travels to a foreign land and learns to survive in and influence the big world. Classic Heroes are Neo in *The Matrix* and Luke Skywalker in *Star Wars*.

Together, the Virgin and the Hero represent the processes of knowing yourself as an individual, internally and externally. They also represent the two halves of having a relationship with your self: self-fulfillment and self-sacrifice.

From a power perspective, the Virgin and the Hero are moving from knowing themselves as dependent on people to knowing their own power. The Virgin gains the power to be all that she can be. It is the power to fulfill her greatest potential. The Hero gains the power to overcome his fear and shape and protect his world, even against the will of others.

The Virgin and the Hero represent the positive aspects of taking up individual power. Both separate themselves from the power structures they are born into such as being the daughter or son of... or the religious traditions of... and find a power they have earned through their own actions. The Virgin creates an emotional separation while the Hero separates himself physically from the people on which he was once dependent.

The Whore and the Coward represent the shadow side of failing to take up individual power. The Whore is caught in a life that services the needs, values, and directions of others, to her own detriment and neglect. The Coward is so fearful of death that his life occupies a very small space.

The Virgin and the Whore carry the values of their community. As a shadow side, the Whore represents what is of low value. She is often seen as dirty, used, debased, weak, pathetic, and ruined beyond repair. Her sexuality is a metaphor for her spiritual essence or soul that is used in the service of others. The Whore is selling her soul to conform to the expectations of others. She is the scapegoat: blamed for all manner of sins and then run out of town literally or emotionally through the shaming and shunning of her and her bastard children. Societal judgments promote a downward spiral for the Whore into a complete loss of self and isolation, depression, insanity, or suicide. Anne Boleyn plays the Whore as she complies with her family's plan to gain social power in *The Other Boleyn Girl*.

The Whore is selling her soul because she is completely out of touch with it or because she feels like a victim who lacks the power of an individual. The selling of the Whore's soul does not have to be sexual. The husband who feels powerless to leave a self-destructive marriage because of low self-esteem, or the worker who hates her job because she has no personal expression also embody this shadow archetype. Belle in *Beauty and the Beast* plays the Whore when she exchanges her life for her father's and then devotes herself to the transformation of the Beast (Zipes, 37).

The Coward fails to explore the world beyond his safe village and therefore has no confidence he can survive on his own. He lies, cheats, shirks, and bullies people to avoid being challenged in his ability to provide for himself. He avoids anything that could lead to death or the fear of death or even hardship. Cypher (*The Matrix*) is the ultimate Coward when he betrays the last settlement of free humans because he wants the comforts of ignorance. He wants to be rich and have good food and a comfy bed. Raymond Shaw in *The Manchurian Candidate (1962)* is another good example of the Coward archetype where his notorious failure to separate from his mother makes him an ideal candidate for brainwashing.

These shadow archetypes are doomed to believe they must stay attached to other people to survive. The Whore believes she must appease or please people and is thereby a victim. The Coward believes he must control others to survive, and is a bully or an eternal child.

TABLE 1. Comparison of the Archetypal Features of the Virgin, Whore, Hero, and Coward

	Virgin	Whore	Hero	Coward
stage	beginning	beginning	beginning	beginning
relationship	to self	to self	to self	to self
boundary	internal	internal	external	external
drive	self-fulfillment	self-deprivation	self-sacrifice	self-preservation
highest purpose	to be authentic and know joy	to be insane and depressed	to be brave and develop skills	to be attached to comfort and security
power	empowered to be everything she is capable of	no personal power; slave; victim	the power to shape the world even against the will of others	small sphere of existence, bully, eternal child

The Mother/Goddess, the Lover/King, the Femme Fatale and the Tyrant are the four archetypes who represent the middle stage of life, and all face the challenge of entering into a relationship with another. This is the search for the sacred union of the feminine with the masculine, at the risk of losing oneself.

The Mother/Goddess and the Lover/King know their power and must now enter into a relationship to use their power well and gain meaning in their life. This relationship can be between a man and a woman, a mother or a father and a child, and a woman or a man and her/his community. This union brings a form of wholeness.

The Mother/Goddess knows her power and is using her talent to nurture and inspire others, gradually depleting her resources. She must find a home for her power which rejuvenates her or she will burn out. To do this she must develop the art of receiving another into her heart and her life. Vianne, in the movie *Chocolat*, is seen as a threat to patriarchy as she brings sensuality and pleasure to her new village. When the battle for acceptance exhausts Vianne, the villagers open themselves to her ways and create a new type of community that embraces her. Pepa in *Women on the Verge of a Nervous Breakdown*, Antonia in *Antonia's Line*, Lotty in *Enchanted April* and Daniel in *Mrs. Doubtfire* all portray this essence of the Mother/Goddess archetype.

The Lover/King is challenged to surrender his heart to the feminine. However, attaching to the feminine renders him vulnerable to the mini-death of rejection if he is found unworthy, or to the vulnerability created by loving someone, providing his enemies with a means of inflicting death-like pain on him by harming his loved one. He also fears misplacing his love and meeting his emotional death at the hands of the Femme Fatale.

The Lover/King must face this fear, and even experience the death of some aspect of himself, in order to be reborn and have meaning and purpose in his life. In so doing, he becomes the dying and rising god. Through the experience of joining the feminine and the masculine or allowing love to become central to life, the Lover/King gains a form of immortality. He goes from living in black and white to living in Technicolor.

In *Michael Clayton*, Michael has an opportunity to acquire a large sum of money but chooses instead to expose evil and make the world a better place for his son. Michael rises above his past to reveal his better self to his son. In the movie *Camelot*, King Arthur must choose between standing by Guinevere, even when she has fallen in love with another man, or sacrificing her according to the code of his men. Arthur aligns himself with his men, the kingdom falls apart, and Arthur is a broken man.

The Bridges of Madison County, The Terminal, and *Casino Royale* contain strong images of the Lover/King archetype and his struggle with creating a relationship with the feminine.

The Mother/Goddess has the power to nurture, inspire, create ecstasy, and bring chaos. She uses her power to create growth and unconditional love in others. The Lover/King has the power to assert his will over others, even against their will, and bring integrity, order, justice, and security to his community. The Lover/King and the Mother/Goddess must come together to harmonize their powers to bring a balance of growth and stability, nurturance and justice, and receiving and offering.

The Femme Fatale and the Tyrant fail in the quest to join the feminine and the masculine by using people to preserve and enhance themselves. The Femme Fatale embodies a manipulative misuse of emotional power resulting in emasculation, dehumanization, and mistrust. These are all major impediments to entering into a loving relationship. In the movie *Chicago*, Roxie kills her lover, who told her he actually couldn't get her into vaudeville, and tries to pin it on her husband, Amos. Amos believes his wife when she says the man was a burglar and willingly confesses to the murder. When he learns the guy has been visiting three times a week, he feels like a sap and rescinds his confession. Roxie accuses him of being a bad husband.

The Tyrant seeks to use his power for personal gain and is unfeeling towards the feminine. The Tyrant believes in transactional giving – he gives to get. He aims to control and dominate others. *The Godfather* movies enter the world of the Tyrant with murderous behavior in the name of the family. Codes stress the importance of respecting the Godfather's dominance and superiority, and every interaction must give the Tyrant a benefit of status, respect, money, power, or future considerations.

The Femme Fatale and the Tyrant wish to maintain an imbalance of power. The Femme Fatale wants to emotionally manipulate the masculine until he is castrated. She sucks the life energy of others until they are dead. The Tyrant wants to assert his will over others to his maximum gain. He dominates a world of usury, rape, crime, violence, and patriarchal codes.

TABLE 2. Comparison of the Archetypal Features of the Mother/Goddess, Femme Fatale, Lover/King, and Tyrant

	Mother/Goddess	Femme Fatale	Lover/King	Tyrant
stage	middle	middle	middle	middle
relationship	to another	to another	to another	to another
boundary	internal	internal	external	external
drive	to inspire love and growth in others	to control the emotions and energy of others	to provide order, justice and security for others	to induce criminal behavior, usury and terror in others
highest purpose	to receive another human being into her heart	to suck another's life energy until s/he dies	to extend service to another human being	transactional giving for net personal gain
power	to create growth and love in others	to manipulate emotions for personal gain	to provide for and protect others	to control others physically for personal gain

The end stage of life, the time of the Crone, the Hag, the Mentor and the Miser, sees the release of power and attachments to people and things and joining in relationship with the cosmos. The Crone and the Mentor spend their final days on earth releasing their power to leave a positive impact or discovering the beauty in their insignificance.

The Crone looks at the span of a lifetime and uses this perspective to recognize the growth people need to undergo when they can't see it themselves. This growth initially appears to be a hardship, but eventually proves to be a transformation that makes life meaningful. The Crone's abilities approach the magical as she moves towards releasing her body form and joining the spiritual world. She is the Trickster, using magic, intuition, and serendipity to drive people to face their flaws, as in *Beauty and the Beast*, where the old woman curses the Prince to be a beast until he learns to love and be loved in return. Fiona Anderson in *Away From Her* and Ninny Threadgoode in *Fried Green Tomatoes* also represent this journey of the Crone where the old woman places a friend in a situation that challenges the friend to grow.

The Mentor reflects on his life and evaluates his value to humanity. He looks for ways to leave a lasting memory of his time on earth after his physical body is gone. He endows gifts, builds monuments to things he values, supports causes he deems worthy and transfers his knowledge and wisdom to worthy recipients. He ensures the continuation of stability and good values through philanthropy, building, and mentoring and in this way gains a form of immortality.

The Hag and the Miser refuse to enter into a relationship with the cosmos. The Hag refuses to accept her unused potential and uses her magic to deny aging and confound the pathway of others. She may divert a Lover/King from his true destiny and into a hopeless union with her. Rather than contributing to the next generation, she robs it of a future. Mrs. Robinson in *The Graduate* is the perfect model of a Hag, as are Sheba Hart and Barbara Covett in *Notes on a Scandal*. The Hag is also the harbinger of doom, spreading a pessimistic message of the hopelessness of the future, as Hanna does in *The Reader*.

The power of the Hag is to cause stagnation in the personal growth of others. She cripples people with fear or interrupts their growth by using her magic to inhabit their lives. Brook and Mel in *Thirteen* are examples of the Hag who confounds the lives of teenage girls, consumed with efforts to appear young rather than fulfilling their mother role. Marquise Isabelle de Merteuil and Vicomte Sebastien de Vamont in *Dangerous Liaisons* also embody the Hag interfering in the lives of others for their personal amusement.

The Miser refuses to see the value of his accumulations to the greater community, even though power and material things are becoming of limited use to him. He hoards his wealth for himself and ignores the effect of his neglect on others. The actions of the Miser make his time spent on earth quickly forgotten. The classic example of the Miser is Scrooge in *A Christmas Carol*. The Miser also permits ignorance, neglect, deprivation, and instability in the community. The father who is too busy working to engage with his children, as seen in movies like *Thirteen* and *Liar Liar*, embodies this archetype.

TABLE 3. **Comparison of the Archetypal Features of the Crone, Hag, Mentor, and Miser**

	Crone	Hag	Mentor	Miser
stage	end	end	end	end
relationship	to cosmos	to cosmos	to cosmos	to cosmos
boundary	internal	internal	external	external
drive	to shake up people's lives to force their transformation	to interfere with people's lives to avoid their transformation	to give gifts of wisdom, sword, money, knowledge	to neglect others, and have more for himself
highest purpose	to cause growth in others and join the cosmos	to cause stagnation in others and deny the existence of the cosmos	to endow gifts on worthy recipients and leave a lasting positive effect on the world	to amass wealth for himself and ignore deprivation, ignorance and instability
power	magic to encourage self-fulfillment in others	emotional manipulation to cause stagnation in others	tools to ensure future safety and stability in the community	walls to separate himself from the community

The Language of Symbols

Writers know the adage "Show, don't tell." This phrase points to a fundamental feature of archetypes: they speak through symbols. On-the-nose dialogue addresses the brain. Symbols address the unconscious and the soul of people, which is much more powerful and engaging than an appeal to the brain. Carl Jung recognized that archetypes are moved from our unconscious to our consciousness through symbols (Jung, 1976, 321), which explains why film is such a powerful medium for the expression of archetypal stories: it can be embedded with a wealth of symbols.

Metaphors are word images rather than words of direct meaning. In *Billy Elliot*, for example, the writer could address the brain with Billy saying, "I am struggling to find a place for my feminine energy which needs to be expressed through dance, and I need you to accept this part of me and not assume I'm gay. Mom would." Instead we are given dialogue and images of Billy caring for and feeding his grandmother, who is undervalued by the men; sitting at his deceased mother's piano, trying to play the piano and being rebuffed by his dad; hating boxing classes, which his father highly values; coming alive in dancing classes; and watching his father bust up his mother's piano to burn for heat. The words and pictures that speak symbolically have a much more powerful effect, even though they send the same message as the direct words. A symbol holds more meaning than words can explicitly state and opens up new avenues for understanding (Jung, 1976, 307).

Jung wrote, "Meaning only comes when people feel they are living the symbolic life, that they are actors in the divine drama" (Hollis, 2004, 11). This statement ties into another fundamental principle of screenwriting — audiences need a protagonist they can relate to. Virgins and Heroes are symbols for the universal need to stand on your own. When a symbol connects with the unconscious it generates energy that makes a person feel alive and ready to take on a transformation (Stein, 81). This is when character arc occurs. "When we resonate to this incarnated energy, we know we are in the presence of Soul" (Hollis, 1995, 9), and it gives the power to overcome hardship. The key to writing strong, relatable characters is finding symbols that personify the archetypes and make them recognizable.

The essential three acts of life appear in our culture as the trinities. They are the Holy Trinity of the Father, the Son, and the Holy Ghost, or the Celtic Trilogy of the Maiden, the Mother and the Crone. Each of these has a shadow counterpart, making twelve core archetypes. These essential archetypes can be known by many names. There may also be other archetypes that function beyond these twelve, but they represent the minimum a screenwriter needs to be familiar with. Table 4 includes examples of the range of male and female descriptive names in each category.

TABLE 4. **Various Names Associated with the Twelve Core Archetypes**

	Feminine Archetypes		Masculine Archetypes	
	light	*shadow*	*light*	*shadow*
beginning	princess, prince, virgin, maiden, artist, rebel, little-train-that-could, magical child	whore, victim, slave, prostitute, sad clown	hero, heroine, adventurer, liberator, rescuer, avenger, saviour, cowboy	coward, bully, eternal child
middle	mother, father, goddess, god, healer, storyteller, priestess, Samaritan	femme fatale, vampire, wicked stepmother, bitch/manipulator,	lover, king, queen, warrior, mediator, judge, angel, advocate	tyrant, evil queen, dictator, destroyer
end	crone, fairy godmother, trickster, fool, jester, shape-shifter, mystic alchemist	hag, lecher, thief, saboteur, cougar, gossip, Don Juan	wise man, wise woman, philanthropist, benefactor	miser, spinster, hermit

Archetypal journeys are not one-time events which occur at a certain age. Each time a social organization places someone at odds with their true nature, the Virgin archetype provides guidance towards becoming authentic. Any time something valued is threatened the Hero archetype may rise to save it. These moments can happen at any age and any number of times in a story.

Also, a character is not restricted to embodying a single archetype. The Virgin may play the Whore for a while, to emphasize the consequences of not realizing her dream. The Hero may play the Virgin as seen when a Prince is frustrated by the duties he is born to. Each archetype, however, represents a pivotal transformation and a protagonist generally follows one major journey.

Comparison of the Virgin and Hero

Virgin and Hero stories explore the theme of knowing yourself as an individual. Jung defined individuation as "the personal struggle for consciousness," which begins with the understanding that you can exist as an individual (Stein, 174). The Virgin frees herself from dependency on her family of origin by connecting to her inner world. She expands her values to include her personal choice by developing her sensuality, creativity, and spirituality in a drive towards joy. The Hero achieves a sense of his ability to exist in the larger world by travelling to a strange land without anyone to provide food, shelter and safety for him and by challenging evil. He is learning to be brave, clever, skilled, strong, and rugged in a drive to overcome his fear of death.

The Virgin and the Hero story patterns are in many ways polar opposites of one another, two halves that make up a whole. Although they are both stories of learning to stand alone, the Virgin story is about knowing her dream for herself and bringing it to life while surrounded by the influences of her kingdom (*Ever After*). The Hero story is about facing mortal danger by leaving his village and proving he can exist in a larger world (*Willow*). The Virgin shifts her values over the course of her story to fully be herself in the world. The Hero is focused on developing his skills to actively do things that need to be done in the world. The Virgin is about self-fulfillment, while the Hero is about self-sacrifice. They represent the two driving forces in humans when faced with challenges: propelled towards the joy of being in harmony with yourself (Virgin's journey); or driven away from fear to face hardship and conquer it bravely (Hero's journey).

In Jungian terms, the Virgin must overcome her Father, or Ophelia, Complex, which is a need to please and conform to others' values. Ophelia, in Shakespeare's *Hamlet*, is a young, sheltered girl who is used by her father to gain information about Prince Hamlet after he notices Hamlet is drawn to Ophelia's beauty. A pawn to her father, superficially loved and later considered a whore by Hamlet, Ophelia eventually goes insane.

The Ophelia story illustrates the theme of how the Virgin must stop conforming to the wishes or beliefs of others or suffer greatly. Dependent on her father for love and security, and therefore unwilling to disturb his world of tradition, commerce, protection, and order, Ophelia adapts to her father's values at the expense of her own.

The Virgin may even be proud to be useful to her father and enjoy his attention. Her over-identification with father-centered values will eventually leave her feeling empty until her own instincts towards creativity, sexuality or spirituality begin to rise. These feminine qualities make the father uncomfortable because they threaten his ordered world. The Virgin learns that she must place her own values and vision for her life ahead of those of her father (Murdock, xiii, 89) as seen in *Bollywood/Hollywood* and *Billy Elliot*.

The vision the Virgin has for herself could be a choice of lover, one who adores her rather than one who meets societal expectations of sexual orientation or social status (*Brokeback Mountain* and *Shakespeare in Love).* She may dream of being a dancer, crusader, singer, soccer player, or boxer while her family, school or social class disapprove (*Strictly Ballroom, Erin Brockovich, Bend It Like Beckham*). She may have a spiritual need to reach for a sports achievement against impossible odds (*Rocky, Angels in the Outfield*). She must look inside herself and reach for her dream regardless of what others envision for her.

The Hero's journey is the path to overcoming his Mother, or Oedipal, Complex, which is a desire to cling to the comforts of home at the expense of knowing the bigger world. In Sophocles' *Oedipus the King,* Oedipus is a tragic character who inadvertently kills his father and marries his mother. This cautionary tale warns of the dangers of not separating from the place of origin.

The Hero must overcome his trepidations about leaving the warmth of the village, the metaphoric womb, and venture into the unknown to face his fear of death. He will only truly know that he can stand alone once he has proven himself in a foreign and inhospitable land. The Hero is motivated by the need to keep the village (or the maternal) safe but ultimately gains the knowledge that he has the skill to beat back death and live autonomously.

The differences between the Virgin and Hero themes illustrate the internal and external aspects of the process of knowing yourself as an individual. The Virgin emotionally separates from the people with whom she lives and creates a boundary between their values and hers while still living with them. The Hero physically detaches from the comforts of home and derives power from knowing hardship and developing skills. These archetypal stories show the path to becoming individuals, emotionally or psychologically and physically.

The Virgin and the Hero symbolize two aspects of knowing one's place in the world. The archetypal journey takes the protagonist from one polarity to the other, from shadow to light. Growth initiates from the Whore or the Coward, and then follows a path into the Virgin and Hero journeys. Therefore, the Virgin begins her story lacking a sense of self, giving too much energy to the needs and opinions of others. In the end, the Virgin meets her need for self-fulfillment. By contrast, the Hero starts with a strong sense of self-preservation, refusing to get involved. Ultimately, he meets his duty of service to others through self-sacrifice.

Another major distinction between the Virgin and Hero stories is the setting. The Virgin transforms within her kingdom; the familiar domestic setting where people assume they know what is best for her. This setting sets up the task for the Virgin to assert her vision for her life against the psychological pull of her community.

The Virgin does not leave her kingdom because her challenge is to face the influences of her domestic world whether they are physically around her or in her head. She finds a **Secret World** within her kingdom in which to practice her dream and grow in strength. At the same time, she meets the expectations of her **Dependent World**, keeping both worlds alive for as long as she can, fearful of discovery, yet joyful in her developing dream. If the Virgin does leave the kingdom, the internal pressures that limit her actions must be portrayed in some other way, such as flashbacks or incidents that refer to an earlier influence that still affects her.

The Hero story is set in a foreign land — the more foreign, the better. It can be another country, galaxy or social status, but everything he experiences is unfamiliar, such as habits, food, customs, and clothing. When he enters this land he is marked as an outsider, vulnerable to any number of unknown dangers. Danger is a key element because the Hero is pushing the boundaries of his mortality, exploring how far he can risk his life and still survive. Notably, the Hero has no feeling for the world he enters beyond fear and curiosity. He feels exposed, and there is no movement back and forth between the comforts of home and the hardships of his new surroundings.

The kingdom of the Virgin and the village of the Hero also undergo different experiences during the individuation of these characters. The kingdom is thrown into chaos by the Virgin and will undergo fundamental change as a result of her path. Usually, some aspect of the kingdom is causing stagnation among its people but they are so attached to order that they go along with an evil force or block individual growth to maintain it. The transformation of the Virgin will result in a change in the way people in her kingdom live, despite their initial resistance. The process of change usually occurs as a shift in attitudes or practices, rather than a physical destruction of property – unless, of course, the Hero shows up and eliminates an evil by force. In either case, this change will prove to be a benefit to the kingdom.

The Hero's village, on the other hand, is seen as essentially good, if perhaps boring and too comfortable. It is worthy of preservation and will remain fundamentally unchanged, thanks to the efforts of the Hero. As the Hero undergoes his journey, the only change for the village is the elimination of the threat of danger. The foreign land doesn't fare as well. While the Hero is in the foreign land, he is unconcerned about causing hurt feelings or property damage.

The kingdom of the Virgin represents the parts of a community that are in need of change. The village of the Hero represents what is good in a community and worth preserving. Together the actions of the Virgin and the Hero provide the balance of growth and stability in a community.

The obstacle in the Virgin story is the people around her who want to control her actions. The Virgin is not a volunteer in this adventure; rather, the plan for her life is the central theme. No one is encouraging her to take action: in fact, they are strongly discouraging it. While the kingdom wants her to be passive, the Virgin wants to actively pursue her own path.

In contrast, the village is the target of the evil in the Hero's journey. The Hero volunteers to battle this evil, making himself an obstacle to evil, but he is not the intended target. To emphasize this point, the Hero begins by refusing the call to adventure (*Unforgiven* and *Romancing the Stone*). The village wants the Hero to be active but he must volunteer to be self-sacrificing. In this way, the Virgin and the Hero have a very different relationship to the hardship that blocks their individuation processes.

The attitude of the Virgin and the Hero toward their obstacle is also different. The obstacle for the Virgin may be her love for the people of the kingdom, those who wish to keep her from changing. And it is their love for her that eventually brings change to their view of the Virgin and the kingdom as a whole. The growth of the antagonist out of love for the Virgin is often a major feature of the story. The obstacle does not need to be evil. It may be misguided, mistaken, overprotective or unknowingly living through the Virgin.

In the Hero story, the obstacle is evil. The Hero understands that it must be destroyed, neutralized, or eliminated. Things are separated more clearly into good and evil in the Hero's journey. The antagonist usually does not grow in a Hero story: he is killed.

Stories of the Virgin and the Hero show ways to take up personal power. They do not, however, define power in the same way. The definition of power, according to sociologist Max Weber (which I would characterize as a masculine perspective), is "the chance for a man, or a number of men, to realize their own will in a communal action even against the will of others who are participating in the action"; or "the ability of a person to impose his will upon others despite resistance" (Wallimann, 231). Power is synonymous with control, command, jurisdiction, authority, and might.

This perspective on power is built around group control. The goal of the group takes precedence over the desires of an individual or a group asserts its will over another group. Sometimes the Hero asserts his will against a group but always on behalf of others. The Hero goes against evil, alone or with a group, asserts his will for the good of his village, and gains a sense of his power.

Another definition of power, put forward in the video *Women: A True Story: 2, The Power Game* offers a feminine definition of power, which is more appropriate for the Virgin. The word "power" may have originated from the Latin word *posse*, which was defined as "to be all that we are capable of being." This feminine definition of power is more individual-based and captures the essence of power in the phrase "the power of love." It is about an individual fully coming into being, without imposing her will on others.

The Virgin pursues the art of fully "Being" and comes into her power when she sorts through all the seeds of her values and lives her life accordingly (Woodman, 78). She overcomes the masculine power that is controlling her, but not by doing battle with those asserting their will against hers. She reveals her inner self and inspires people to change through their love for her, their desire for the same autonomy, or the recognition of the value she brings. She and others are propelled towards change by the valuing of joy.

The quest of the Virgin is to become all she is capable of being and in so doing create joy and happiness. The quest of the Hero is to assert his will against evil and in so doing overcome fear. Becoming an individual is the process of coming into one's personal power, in both its feminine and masculine aspects.

There is also a difference in the roles of the supporting characters within the Virgin and Hero stories. The characters in a Virgin story are people who are out of balance. The people she loves are often the ones blocking her from following her passion. These characters grow and change with the Virgin. Hero story characters are more dualistic, clearly either good or evil. The importance of the battle of good against evil is emphasized by the tragic death of minor, truly good characters, but overall, good triumphs.

Also, the Virgin has old friends while the Hero has new allies. In the Virgin story there is often a childhood friend who stands by the Virgin and unconditionally loves her. The girlfriend in *Working Girl* or *Maid in Manhattan* and the family servants in *Ever After* are typical of the Virgin supporting characters. The friends are reflections of the Virgin's value, foreshadowing her potential from an early stage.

The supporting characters in the Hero story are allies met along his journey who share the common goal of defeating evil. Classic examples include the Tin Man, Scarecrow, and the Cowardly Lion in *The Wizard of Oz* or Princess Leia and Han Solo in *Star Wars*. Their bond is based on their common mission. It is not necessary that allies like each other as long as there is mutual interest.

Two other archetypes, the Mentor and the Crone, have similar functions in both stories. They give that extra help that tips the balance in favor of success for the Virgin or the Hero. The Crone uses magic or trickery as the High Aldwin does in *Willow* and the boy with the mouse does in *Shakespeare in Love*. The Mentor provides tools, wisdom and knowledge as Gandalf does in *Lord of the Rings* and Morpheus does in *The Matrix*.

The tensions are also different in the Virgin and Hero stories. The cost of the Virgin going on her pathway is the potential loss of love, joy, and passion. Without these things that accompany the fulfillment of her dream, the Virgin suffers loss of self, which manifests as depression, insanity or suicide. The cost to the Hero of going on his journey is potentially death. This loss of life at the hands of others will involve physical pain and leave his village vulnerable to evil.

Both stories follow an emotional pattern in which the protagonist is at first tenuous, then takes a chance and almost loses, but learns from this experience and finally follows the pathway to success. In short, they both go through emotional reversals that make for great storytelling.

TABLE 5. Comparison of the Virgin and Hero Stories

	Virgin	Hero
Drive	to know joy	to overcome fear
Individuation	resolution of the Father Complex; separate emotionally or psychologically; develop personal values	resolution of the Mother Complex; separate physically; develop skills
Boundaries	internal	external
Qualities	creativity, sensuality, spirituality self-fulfillment	bravery, strength, ruggedness self-sacrifice
Setting	domestic realm	foreign land
Genre	fairy tales	myths
Effect on Community	chaos and change	stability and safety
Supporting Characters	friends	allies
Relation to Power	individual focus; to be all that you are capable of being; to be	group focus; to assert your will, even against the will of others; to do
Effect of Failure	insanity, depression, suicide	death, cowardice

Chapter 2

The Virgin Archetypal Journey

he essence of the Virgin story is that she must follow her dream or authentic nature despite the wishes of others. The path to realizing that dream follows universal stages or beats. The beats form both the character arc and the actions that symbolically represent the archetypal transformation. Altogether the beats of the Virgin story are:

1. Dependent World
2. Price of Conformity
3. Opportunity to Shine
4. Dresses the Part
5. Secret World
6. No Longer Fits Her World
7. Caught Shining
8. Gives Up What Kept Her Stuck
9. Kingdom in Chaos
10. Wanders in the Wilderness
11. Chooses Her Light
12. Re-Ordering (Rescue)
13. The Kingdom Is Brighter

Stage One: Dependent World

The Virgin's journey begins with an introduction to the world on which she is dependent, the world in which a part of her is lying dormant. The **Dependent World** is an external authority that provides for the Virgin's existence. It can be a parental, familial, cultural, or spiritual world that the Virgin landed in before she knew independent choice.

The **Dependent World** may be well intentioned or evil in nature. Even if it is well intentioned, authority has a tendency to exclude its opposite and will eventually become an oppressor (Hollis, 2004, 47). The Virgin is attached to this world in some way. It may be a tangible attachment or a memory from a past experience that governs her behavior today. This dependent attachment may also be a two-way street. People around the Virgin may be dependent on her. In either case, the Virgin finds herself in a **Dependent World** where others control her future.

Generally Virgin stories occur in the domestic realm, which becomes a metaphor for the influences on her decision-making process. The more control the kingdom has over her movements, the more control it has over her thoughts and values.

The Virgin doesn't have to stay in this domestic world to undergo her archetypal journey as long as she carries its values with her. Mulan leaves home and joins the army (*Mulan*). The army continues the values of her culture regarding the roles and restrictions placed on women. Mulan's safety is dependent on the army not discovering she is a girl. The penalty set by her culture, and acknowledged by her family, is death.

Alternatively, the values could be carried by a photograph (image) of an elder, as in *Bend It Like Beckham* and *Bollywood/ Hollywood*. The protagonist may hear messages from the elder image and talk to the photo in times of struggle. Memories also establish the **Dependent World** of the Virgin in *While You Were Sleeping*.

The **Dependent World** in a Virgin story is the impediment to her self-realization, otherwise known as the antagonist. On one level it is a force within her kingdom. On another, it is a belief the Virgin holds which keeps her attached to her **Dependent World**.

There are four common scenarios that establish the Virgin's dependency. These include being dependent on others for material survival, by social convention, for protection, and by the need for love.

Dependent on Others for Material Survival

The simplest way to establish the Virgin's dependence on others is to have a young protagonist whose survival still rests in the hands of other people. In *Billy Elliot*, for example, Billy is just a kid. His mother is dead and he has to take care of his grandmother while his father and brother go to work, establishing a hierarchy of dependence. Billy has to endure masculine dominance, as portrayed by his father's insistence he take boxing lessons, and his father and brother's masculine communication style, because they are the only family he has left. In *Little Miss Sunshine*, Olive has to live within the boundaries of her dysfunctional family because she is young and depends on them for a ride to the beauty pageant. Being young automatically makes you dependent.

The connection to others for material survival can be emphasized when the character's environment has extreme conditions such as living in poverty, being orphaned at a young age, or neglected by a parent. In these cases, the Virgin's survival is precarious. Cinderella and Snow White, for example, have lost at least one parent and must ingratiate themselves with a servant or appease a stepmother for survival.

In *Angels in the Outfield*, Rodger exemplifies a state of tenuous survival when his father puts him up for adoption. Rodger depends on his father growing up in order to have a biological family. He later becomes a ward of the state, depending on a stranger to choose him for a family placement.

Vivian (*Pretty Woman*) has limited ability to provide for herself, with no connections, no education, and low self-esteem. Vivian turns to prostitution to provide for the food and shelter she needs to survive.

The opposite extreme, living with material excess, is another scenario in which dependency is created. There is a shadow side to the pampered life. *Clueless*, *Legally Blond*, and *About a Boy* have protagonists who are dulled to their personal goals because everything is provided for them. They develop high material needs and depend on others to meet them.

In *Legally Blond*, Elle is expected to be beautiful, fun, and not serious. Her culture has instilled in her that her life goal is to marry a rich man. This belief becomes her **Dependent World**. Will (*About a Boy*) won't risk failure or embarrassment when he can be kept in high style by his father's royalties. Will's **Dependent World** is his theory of being an island to avoid the humility he witnessed his father go through as an aspiring songwriter.

Geography can also be a factor in creating the **Dependent World**. Pocahontas, in *Pocahontas*, lives in a village in the woods. The communal nature of her existence, necessitated by geographic isolation, makes her dependent upon her people. Moonie, in *New Waterford Girl*, lives an isolated existence in the small mining town of Cape Breton, a place where people have survived for generations by sticking together. Inhospitable to diversity, her community requires her to conform to belong.

DEPENDENT ON OTHERS BY SOCIAL CONVENTION

Cultural ceremonies and traditions are designed to form strong bonds that influence people's actions. These cultural values give members a shared sense of meaning that is often instrumental to their survival. The community depends on the Virgin for the continuation of these traditions because she is vested with the future responsibility of cooking, celebrating, birthing, and raising children. She is the vehicle by which traditions are transmitted. Her desire to follow a dream of her own is a threat to tradition as seen in *Whale Rider.*

The urgency of continuing cultural practices is heightened for immigrant families who face the threat of losing their traditions to the host culture. *Bend It Like Beckham* is an example of this kind of dependency. The mother needs Jas to learn how to cook a full Indian dinner. The whole family must conform to traditional Indian values for Jas's sister to be marriageable.

The transfer of wealth through dowry practices and marriage is another form of social convention that makes the family dependent on the Virgin. In *The Other Boleyn Girl, Pride & Prejudice,* and *Bollywood/Hollywood,* it is easy to understand the pressure to marry well and secure the family fortune. The Virgin becomes a pawn in the transference of power and money.

Dependent World in *The Other Boleyn Girl*

In *Bollywood/Hollywood,* Sue is driven to "chatting up" men in bars by her outrage at being treated like chattel for her father's benefit. Yet, her action shows her deep attachment to her father, otherwise known as her Father Complex. Whether she is using her life to please her father or using it to displease him, it makes no difference. She is still living in the world of his values rather than defining her own values.

Definitions of gender roles are another social convention that limits people in their quest for self-expression. In *The Full Monty*, Gary is an unemployed steelworker who is dependent on gender definitions of manhood, which dictate he must have a job to retain shared custody of his son. The classic example occurs in periods in history where women of middle to upper class were forbidden to work except as governesses and tutors and therefore had little choice but to marry according to their father's wishes, as in *Shakespeare in Love*.

DEPENDENT ON OTHERS FOR PROTECTION

Sometimes the Virgin is in mortal danger by virtue of her relations, making her dependent on others for protection. When there is a remarriage, the Virgin becomes competition for the King's love and may need protection from her stepmother.

The envious stepmother has power over the Virgin/Princess that is not tempered by maternal love. The power aspect of their relationship is further heightened when the stepmother is also the Queen, as in *Snow White*. The Virgin is dependent upon the awareness of the father (who generally won't interfere in household matters), her ability to appease the stepmother, or the love of the servants, to survive.

In the movie retelling of the Cinderella story, *Ever After*, Danielle's father dies only days after bringing his new wife to his estate. As he dies, he turns away from his bride to express his love to Danielle, setting Danielle up for a life of jealous retribution. The envious stepsister is also dangerous as she competes with the Virgin for a father's love. To make matters worse, this is an unequal competition because the stepsister has the love and protection of a mother, as portrayed in *What a Girl Wants*.

The *Snow White* scenario is replayed in *Willow* where the baby, Elora, is pursued by the wicked Queen because the prophecy predicts that Elora will someday usurp the Queen. The Virgin is a defenseless baby in mortal peril and must depend on Willow and Madmartigan for her survival.

The Virgin's association with the King can make her dependent on protection in other ways. In *Roman Holiday*, Princess Anne is a target for shysters because she is the daughter of the King. She could cause the King great embarrassment if she does not control her activities.

At other times the Virgin is a target for kidnapping because she is valuable to the kingdom. The beloved Virgin lives in a **Dependent World** of bodyguards and walls. In *Sister Act*, Deloris is valuable to the police because she was a gangster's girlfriend and witnessed a murder that could put him away if she testifies. Deloris becomes dependent on the witness protection program because of her relationship to the Tyrant. Society is also dependent on Deloris to bring a criminal to justice.

DEPENDENT ON CONDITIONAL LOVE

Finally, there is the love factor. The Virgin is often praised for her goodness and helpfulness. From this, she adopts the belief that love is conditional upon her being compliant and agreeable, as seen in *Dirty Dancing*.

The Virgin may also know the hurt of losing someone she loved and become dependent on emotional defenses to protect her from experiencing that kind of pain again. In *Wedding Crashers*, John lost his parents in childhood. Now he protects himself with superficial relationships to avoid feeling deep emotional pain again.

The attachment seen in *Cinderella*, *Ever After*, and *Pretty Woman*, to name just a few movies, has the Virgin spending her life serving others to secure love. Danielle (*Ever After*) lives under the rules of her stepmother in order to live in her family home among her beloved servants and her father's possessions. She works endlessly to serve her stepmother in the hope that someday she will know the love of a mother. Vivian (*Pretty Woman*) intends to meet Edward's needs so well that he will never let her go. These Virgins believe they will gain happiness and love through serving others. This belief attaches them to others in a way that does not allow their true selves to come to life.

In one form or another, the Virgin is in a dependent situation as she begins her journey.

Stage Two: Price of Conformity

The **Price of Conformity** is the suppression of the Virgin's true self. When the Virgin subscribes to the views of the people around her, she experiences a loss of self. Even when she is aware of what she wants, she doesn't see how she could ever achieve it.

There are four common scenarios in which the Virgin conforms to other people's plans for her life while her own dream stagnates. She may be sleeping through her life, agreeing to live within restrictive boundaries, leading a life of servitude, or facing psychological danger.

SLEEPING THROUGH HER LIFE

One consequence of living in a **Dependent World** is that the Virgin's true nature lies dormant. Her talents and dreams have no expression because she is unaware of them. In *Sleeping Beauty*, Aurora goes from protected and isolated in the woods, not even knowing she is a Princess, to a coma. In a modern version of this story, *While You Were Sleeping*, Lucy is sad and alone for the holidays but she does not actively pursue her dream of being part of a big family and going to Italy. She is passive in her life, living in the memories of her past.

In *About a Boy* and *Clueless*, Will and Cher live in pampered worlds where nothing is expected of them and, in return, they expect nothing of themselves. They have been robbed of the activation energy that comes from the need to earn one's way in the world. It doesn't occur to them to search within themselves to discover their life's purpose. They are asleep to their own potential.

Likewise, Ennis in *Brokeback Mountain* is so emotionally closed, he barely speaks. Traumatized by his father's attitudes towards homosexuality and orphaned at an early age, Ennis is just trying to obtain the basics of food and shelter, and the outward normalcy of having a wife. He has extremely low expectations for joy or love in his life. These potentials lie dormant.

According to Naomi Wolf in *The Beauty Myth*, the societal glorification of women's beauty is another way that women fall prey to the traps of patriarchy (10). As long as females strive to meet an impossible beauty ideal, they will be too busy to get on with other things that might threaten male dominance (16). This is the theme in *Legally Blond*, where Elle is encouraged to use her beauty to get married. Being beautiful, getting married, and not becoming "ugly and serious" are considered Elle's highest life purposes. Until she wakes up and questions the values she is adopting, these tasks keep her from exploring what she might really want from life.

AGREEING TO LIVE WITHIN RESTRICTIVE BOUNDARIES

In another scenario, the Virgin knows her dream, but accepts the restrictive emotional or physical boundaries of her **Dependent World** that make it impossible to realize her dreams.

The emotional barrier to exploring dance is palpable in *Billy Elliot*. Billy takes boxing lessons to be accepted in the masculine world created by his father and brother, even though he hates it. As long as he is conforming to his father's values, there is no room for his love of dancing.

The Virgin may make her dream smaller to keep it acceptable to her **Dependent World**, or back down when she is denied avenues to follow her dream. This is often the case when the Virgin is attached to others by social convention or for physical safety.

Scott, in *Strictly Ballroom*, is heavily pressured by the dance community to perform in a conventional way despite his intense desire to try new steps in competition. He complies with their belief that he can win only if he does the standard steps and implicitly accepts that winning is the ultimate goal, rather than attempting to reach his personal potential as a dancer.

In the classic Father Complex, the daughter adopts her father's values to secure her position with him. Her attitudes regarding her body, her creativity, her spirituality, and her intimacy with others are suppressed or reframed to preserve her father's love for her (Murdock, *xv*). Jas, in *Bend It Like Beckham*, wants to play organized soccer. However, it is considered unsuitable for an Indian woman to expose her legs and make an exhibition of herself, much less neglect her duties of cooking and marrying. Jas played soccer as long as it was the hobby of a girl. Furthermore, Jas suppresses her passion to appease her father's belief that he has to protect her from prejudice by limiting her world.

Price of Conformity in *Bend It Like Beckham*

Stereotypes can also create restrictive boundaries. In *Maid in Manhattan*, Marisa's dream is to rise from a chambermaid to a management position in a large hotel organization. She is hampered by her mother's belief that people of their class and cultural background don't aspire beyond cleaning other people's houses. As a single mom and immigrant, Marisa accommodates her mother's views to keep the peace.

In *Sister Act,* the boundaries are more physical as Deloris accepts living in a convent to keep her gangster boyfriend from knocking her off before she can testify against him. Deloris finds convent life restrictive and her dream of becoming a performer appears to have no place to grow. In *Aladdin,* Jasmine is confined to the walls of the palace for her safety. Her dream of exploring the outside world has no outlet when she accepts these boundaries.

Experiencing envy is a great motivator for finding protection. Often the Virgin will make herself smaller, or twist herself into a more likeable form, to avoid provoking an envious reaction (Ulanov, 21). This is the case in *Sleeping Beauty* where Aurora remains hidden in the woods because the Evil Fairy threatens her life. Aurora's whole existence has become focused on going unnoticed. As with the other characters mentioned here, Aurora is choosing to live within boundaries set by others.

LIVING A LIFE OF SERVITUDE

Servitude is another **Price of Conformity** for the Virgin. Often, girls are highly praised for being helpful, beautiful, and thoughtful to others. When the reward of love is attached to these behaviors, they become powerful drives. The Virgin is soon so busy meeting the needs of others that there is little time or room to discover her own needs. This is the *Cinderella* scenario.

Danielle, in *Ever After,* is literally a servant to her stepmother and stepsisters, working hard to meet their needs as they fritter away her father's estate. Danielle is serving her stepmother when she really wants to work to create a better form of governance as described in *Utopia,* the last book given to her by her father.

Danielle is also in danger because a lecherous baron wants her to service his needs. When a culture looks to the Virgin to elicit the senses and make them feel alive, she has been given a position of naïve power that others want to control. In *Ever After*, Danielle is desired by the evil baron because she is beautiful and spirited, and this results in her enslavement.

In *The Sound of Music*, Maria is afraid to go out into the world and make her own way. She plans to serve God in the convent as a way of protecting herself from the unknowns of her own interior world and life outside the church walls.

FACING PSYCHOLOGICAL DANGER

The result of a Virgin not responding to her inner purpose can be psychologically dangerous. There is a quote attributed to Jesus in the Gnostic text *The Gospel of Thomas* that describes this idea well: "If you bring forth what is within you, what you bring forth will save you. If you do not bring forth what is within you, what you do not bring forth will destroy you."

When the Virgin finds herself devalued by the people who are supposed to care for her, she internalizes this sense of low self-worth and surrenders her power to those who would use her. It is a step towards entering the shadow side, the Whore, where she completely surrenders authority over her person.

In *Pretty Woman* and *Bollywood/Hollywood*, the Virgin literally sells herself, reflecting her low self-esteem. Vivian states that she turns herself into a robot and "just does it." No feeling. She claims it is easier to believe the "bad stuff" people say about her than to believe in herself. Vivian sells her body when what she really wants to do is go to school and study business.

Moonie, in *New Waterford Girl*, lives in a small Nova Scotia town where everyone obeys the Catholic Church and no one ever moves away. These traditions don't fit with her dream of studying art in New York City. Her pleas to be allowed to go to New York are rejected. In an effort to conform to her family's vision of her future as a nurse, she begins to wear the uniform. This leaves Moonie so out of sorts with her true self that the family doctor puts her on antidepressants.

Movies that feature psychological danger as the price for conforming to the beliefs of others include *Heavenly Creatures* and *The Virgin Suicides*. In these films, the protagonist has become a danger to herself and society. Not fulfilling her dream eats away at the Virgin until she is ill, non-functioning, unpredictable or addicted.

In *Heavenly Creatures*, Juliet and Pauline discover a shared passion for fantasy writing. Neglected by their parents, their **Secret World** becomes all encompassing and they never find a venue for their dreams. Without this opportunity they isolate from their **Dependent World** and become obsessive. They are **Caught Shining** when Pauline is caught in bed with a boy and vilified by her mother, and the parents become disturbed as Juliet and Pauline begin lesbian activity. They are no longer seen as sweet little girls and the parents try to separate them. To preserve their **Secret World** the girls plot the death of Pauline's mother. This is a cautionary tale about the dangers of neglecting the Virgin.

The Virgin Suicides is the story of daughters living under the rule of very strict parents. The **Price of Conformity** is the suicide of a sister with the remaining girls becoming curiosities and examples of a trend rather than being recognized as people in need of serious intervention.

Stage Three: Opportunity to Shine

The **Opportunity to Shine** is the action that leads to the first expression of the Virgin's potential. Through the **Opportunity to Shine**, the Virgin reveals her talent, her dream, or her true nature.

The **Opportunity to Shine** is a compelling event that will not threaten her **Dependent World**, and therefore she goes for it. Sometimes the Virgin believes this opportunity is just a one-time event; sometimes she is convinced that she will not get caught. Either way, the **Opportunity to Shine** reveals tangible proof that the Virgin could bring her dream to reality.

There are several common ways that the **Opportunity to Shine** occurs. It can be directed by fate, actively pursued, a wish fulfilled, a response to someone in need, or the result of a push from the Crone.

DIRECTED BY FATE

Sometimes a series of events take place that put you exactly where you need to be and it is hard to believe that anything but fate is at work. In *While You Were Sleeping* Lucy is a subway ticket-counter employee who dreams of marrying Peter, a handsome commuter she has never even met. Suddenly, Peter is pushed onto the subway tracks and Lucy saves his life. When she is mistaken for his fiancée at the hospital, her journey is launched.

In *Billy Elliot*, the ballet class starts to share space with the boxing class because the striking miners need the ballet studio to meet. When Billy is asked to return the room key to the ballet class, he becomes aware of his dormant desire to dance.

None of the series of events leading to the **Opportunity to Shine** is particularly unusual or even connected to the Virgin's dream, but together they create a situation that compels the Virgin to action.

ACTIVELY PURSUED

Alternatively, the Virgin can actively scheme to create her moment, believing she can take the opportunity and still preserve her **Dependent World**. *Working Girl, Shakespeare in Love,* and *She's the Man* are films where the Virgin knows her dream. In her private moments, she harbors the notion she can make it happen, and one day an opportunity presents itself.

In *Working Girl*, when Tess's boss is stuck in Europe with a broken leg, Tess borrows the boss's life and pretends to be an account executive to regain control of, and promote, her idea. Tess is no longer willing to wait for an invitation to play the game. She uses her boss's absence to actively pursue what she wants.

One common action the Virgin takes is to disguise herself as a boy to enter a world without the confines of being female. Viola wants to act in a Shakespearean play so she dresses as a boy and auditions for the part (*Shakespeare in Love*). She has chosen actions that provide her the **Opportunity to Shine**. However, fate is also working in her favor when an actors' strike creates opportunities for unknown talent.

Opportunity to Shine in *Shakespeare in Love*

In *She's the Man*, when the girls' soccer team is cut before the college scouts get to see Viola play, she dresses as her twin brother to try out for the men's soccer team at another school. She creates the opportunity to be seen by soccer scouts despite what fate dealt her. However, fate has ultimately helped her because playing for the men's team made her a better soccer player. In *She's the Man*, *Shakespeare in Love*, and *Working Girl*, the protagonists believe they can take their **Opportunity to Shine** and not get caught. At the very least, the reward will be greater than the cost.

WISH FULFILLMENT

Wish fulfillment is a kind of hybrid between fate and actively taking a hand in your future. The Virgin appeals to a greater power to make her dream come true. In *Angels in the Outfield,* when Rodger's father likens their chance of becoming a family to the likelihood of the Angels winning the pennant, Rodger wishes on a star. His talent for believing in people comes alive when winged angels start helping out the Angels team on the baseball field.

In *Freaky Friday,* a fortune cookie launches Anna and her mother on a body exchange that will not end until they come to understand each other's perspective. In this movie, a trickster plays a part, along with wish fulfillment, in launching the story.

Wishes are also made over birthday cakes, lucky pennies, and lamps. Anything that has been given a magical property can be used for wish fulfillment.

There is also false wish fulfillment. In *Legally Blond,* when Elle wishes to win Warner back by becoming serious, she gains the motivation to get into Harvard. Once she is there, her true dream emerges and she abandons her wish to marry Warner in favor of becoming a lawyer.

A RESPONSE TO SOMEONE IN NEED

The Virgin can be called to action for a higher purpose that over-shadows the risk of getting caught and losing her **Dependent World**. In a selfless moment, she is inspired by the need of someone else. In *Mulan,* the protagonist is working hard to be a dutiful daughter but she is clearly not suited for a life of obedience and feminine grace. She has a strategic mind and an active nature. When her father is conscripted to fight against the Han because he has no son, Mulan disguises herself as a boy and enlists on his behalf. Her belief that her father faces certain death motivates her to take action.

Danielle, in *Ever After*, is trying to hold together her father's estate when Maurice, one of the servants who helped raise her, is sold. Danielle feels compelled to help Maurice and when fate provides her with the money, she dresses as a courtier and buys him back. This action is in keeping with her true talent of bringing the teachings of the book *Utopia* to life.

Ever After is an example of how more than one vehicle may be invoked for the **Opportunity to Shine.** The combined accident of fate, where Danielle catches the Prince stealing her father's horse and he pays for her silence, and the circumstances of Maurice's peril, create the **Opportunity to Shine.**

In *Wedding Crashers*, when John meets Claire he is inspired by her genuine nature and her need to be well loved. John lowers his defenses to reveal his true nature, hoping to love Claire well. This drive is the initiation of his Virgin journey.

PUSHED BY THE CRONE

The Virgin may be reluctant to pursue her dream and needs a push from the Crone. In the film *Maid in Manhattan*, Marisa's friend submits her application for a hotel management position without Marisa's knowledge. When the job is offered to Marisa, she is forced to take action, rather than passively talk about her dream of working in management.

The dance instructor in *Billy Elliot* recognizes Billy's interest in dance, and rather than ask Billy if he would like to join the class, which would require Billy to make a decision that goes against his father's values, she simply begins to give him instructions. By just following the instructor's orders, Billy's passion for dance finds an expression. Once Billy has awakened his desire to dance it is hard for him to go back to sleep.

Stage Four: Dresses the Part

Dresses the Part provides the viewer with a fun and pleasurable sense that perhaps dreams can come true and life is meant to have joy in it.

But it is not a frivolous event. **Dresses the Part** is a truly magical moment of alchemy. Before the Virgin can consciously relate to the invisible energy of her authentic self, that energy has to be transformed into something tangible (Hollis, 2004, 24). Once her unconscious dream becomes visible, she will never be the same again. The Virgin **Dresses the Part** and becomes beautiful; receives a physical object that she begins to use; participates in a fashion show and knows her potential; or undresses to reveal her true nature.

BECOMES BEAUTIFUL

Every Virgin/Princess is beautiful. It is almost a law. In *The Soul of Beauty*, Ronald Schenk, a Jungian analyst, suggests that true beauty is seen when the soul of a person is reflected in their physical appearance (1994, 38). The Virgin becomes beautiful in **Dresses the Part** and finally exposes the nature of her soul, as a physical expression that others can perceive. The physical manifestation of bringing her authentic nature to life is often described through metaphors of light. Just as the Greek goddess Aphrodite was known for her radiance, the shining forth of an internal quality rather than any physical attribute, the Virgin's beauty is often described in terms of light such as shining, glowing, brilliant, dazzling and iridescent (Schenk, 44, 60). In other words, the Virgin's beauty represents the shining forth of her soul.

Often the Virgin is portrayed as ugly or invisible until she finds a way to express her dream or authentic self. This is the ugly duckling mechanism. In the opening of *Strictly Ballroom*, *Miss Congeniality*, *Pretty Woman* and *Princess Diaries* the Virgin is unattractive. Fran is a mousy and somewhat odd character until she begins to dance with Scott (*Strictly Ballroom*). As Fran develops her expression as a dancer, she becomes visibly more beautiful. In *Miss Congeniality*, Gracie neglects her femininity until she is required to go undercover as a beauty queen to stop a murder plot. Vivian, in *Pretty Woman*, wears a wig and harlot clothes until she is transformed by a make-over that reveals her true nature. *The Princess Diaries* uses the ugly duckling technique, changing Mia's appearance as she steps into the role of a princess. Schenk wrote that beauty is found in the forgotten, discarded, rustic and even obscene (146). All these Virgins/Princesses transform into beauties as they come into themselves. Beauty is a metaphor for being true to your soul.

In *Ever After*, Danielle is merely a servant girl to the Prince until she expresses her opinions concerning *Utopia*. The Prince is surrounded by girls in the latest fashion, makeup, and manners, but it is Danielle who captivates him because she reveals her true nature.

Beauty is also referred to as the aesthetic, which is the opposite of anesthetic as in an induced loss of consciousness or sensation. Experiencing beauty is thought to cause the senses of the receiver to enliven (Tuan, 7). This is what the Virgin does in her sensual role. The color, texture, and shape of her face, body, and fashions express her aliveness. The name Sleeping Beauty is a pairing of the anesthetic and the aesthetic. It foreshadows the need of the Virgin to wake up to her true nature and let it shine in the world.

RECEIVES A PHYSICAL OBJECT

Gaining possession of an object can enable the Virgin to explore her dream. When Billy Elliot is given a pair of ballet shoes, we see him lacing them up and watch them closely as he first explores dance. The dream has gone from being ethereal to something real. Billy is no longer the same little boy he was before this moment; he now has a dream and the means to realize it.

In *Legally Blond,* Elle begins her path as a law student by putting on a pair of black horn-rimmed glasses. These symbolize Elle's ability to see herself as a serious lawyer. Elle wears the glasses again when she is pretending to be a lawyer to help her friend right the injustice of losing her dog. Wearing the glasses gives Elle the confidence to step into the shoes of a lawyer and recognize that law provides a rewarding way to pursue her passion for helping others.

Shirts become a powerful symbol of deep feelings in *Brokeback Mountain.* Following Jack and Ennis's first sexual encounter in *Brokeback Mountain,* Jack is seen naked by the creek washing Ennis's shirt. Later Jack and Ennis have a bloody fistfight before they rejoin society and Jack secretly takes Ennis's shirt. Ennis finds this shirt, smudged with his blood, encased in Jack's shirt in the closet of his childhood home, after Jack's death. Ennis takes the shirts because they symbolize their love. Later, Ennis's daughter visits and asks her father to attend her wedding, giving him a place in her world and society. After she goes, Ennis carefully folds her forgotten jacket and places it in his closet with Jack's shirt, which now hangs inside Ennis's shirt. Potent messages are given through significance placed on these physical objects.

PARTICIPATES IN A FASHION SHOW

The fashion show is a metaphor for the Virgin's ability to experiment with who she really is until she finds the right fit. Sometimes the Virgin is playful and tries a few near misses before finding the right skin. Other times the world objects to her trying to make more of herself and knocks her down but she gets up and tries again. In *Pretty Woman,* Vivian has money but no one on Rodeo Drive will serve her. With the help of Barney, the hotel manager, Vivian finds a dress that reflects her inner beauty, and the Virgin begins to grow into herself.

Once she finds the right outfit, we see the Virgin's potential illuminated. In *Bollywood/Hollywood*, the rebellious Sue tries on traditional Indian dresses and eventually participates in the very wedding traditions she once objected to. This is an interesting juxtaposition. Through it we learn that Sue has a gift for balancing traditional with modern practices and embracing her culture in a new way.

In *Working Girl*, Tess dresses in the sleazy outfit her boyfriend bought her for her birthday, a graphic illustration of the wrong direction her life is taking. Later, Tess tries on several of her boss's dresses until she finds one that gives her the confidence to go to a party and network with her business idea. She risks wearing her boss's dress as a statement that she will no longer devalue herself.

UNDRESSES

In a protected environment, the Virgin may come out of her shell and in dewy nakedness reveal her true self. In *Brokeback Mountain*, Ennis gives up his self-protective nature and gives in to his desire for Jack. He is able to break free of his emotional barriers because he is in the mountains, away from the norms and dangers of cowboy society.

Taking off her maid's uniform in *Maid in Manhattan* allows Marisa to be seen by Chris as a person. Taking off the protective armor, the costume of a hooker, allows the real Vivian to be seen in *Pretty Woman*. In all these examples, the Virgin's true self begins to take shape once she sheds the clothes that fit other people's expectations of her.

Dresses the Part is a tool to help the Virgin grow into her true nature. It shows the importance of the drive towards joy in Virgin stories. It is often in these playful times of freedom that she begins to know her inner self.

Stage Five: The Secret World

Once the Virgin has had a taste of living her dream and has made it a tangible reality, she creates a secret place in which it can thrive. She's not ready to reveal her dream to her **Dependent World** and face the consequences. The Virgin goes back and forth, juggling the impulse to meet the expectations of her **Dependent World** with creating a separate and **Secret World** where she can grow into herself.

In the **Secret World**, the Virgin believes she can find a way to please everyone. The good news is that she has added herself to the list of people who need to be pleased. In **Opportunity to Shine**, her actions were believed to be a one-time event or at least an in-the-moment decision without thought for how it would affect the future. Now this event has led to the creation of a **Secret World** that can be revisited, and she has to find a way to go back and forth between the two worlds. The belief that she can keep them separate and preserve her **Dependent World** is crucial for the Virgin to risk exploring her dream in her **Secret World**.

CREATION OF A SECRET WORLD

The keeping of a secret is a significant step in claiming personal authority. No matter how well intentioned the **Dependent World**, the Virgin must separate from the external authority, be it a parent, a culture, or some kind of tribal deity and come to know her personal authority. This requires some form of rebellion. This process often begins with keeping something secret (Hollis, 2004, 47). Something is protected and given a secure place to exist without seeking approval.

A powerful metaphor for claiming this personal authority to meet one's needs is the Coming of Age story. Exploring sexuality for the first time, compelled by a feeling but unsure of the outcome, needing to do it without seeking permission, and for yourself, is a strong metaphor for the Virgin's need to bring her true nature to reality. In *Do You Remember Dolly Bell?*, Dino hides a new prostitute, Dolly Bell, in his loft for his criminal friends. He explores his desire for her while he tries to figure out life and find acceptance for his belief in magic. In *Stealing Beauty*, Lucy arrives in Italy hoping to discover the identity of her father. Her virginal state is a metaphor for her innocence of the ways of life that led to her unusual parentage and her mother's suicide. Learning the truth of how she came to be is paralleled with her sexual awakening.

Ultimately, discovering her sexuality is a private experience done under the Virgin's own authority. On the shadow side, the experience of the Whore is controlled by someone else in the public domain.

The **Secret World** may also be a physical space, an idea that is only known to some, or a state of mind. The Virgin may be aware from the beginning that her **Secret World** must be private. This is the case in *Ever After*, where Danielle's stepmother has made a habit of keeping close control over her time. In *Brokeback Mountain*, Ennis knows from childhood that his life depends upon not being identified as a homosexual. He and Jack create a separate space in which they can be together.

Secret World in *Brokeback Mountain*

Tess (*Working Girl*) secretly occupies her boss Catherine's office and apartment while Catherine is in hospital. Tess's **Dependent World** exists in the secretary pool and with her high-school friends. Viola, in *Shakespeare in Love*, finds a place where she can act that is defined by wearing the costume of a boy in the theater realm. Scott and Fran find places they can secretly practice in *Strictly Ballroom*. In all these cases a physical space defines the **Secret World**.

In other cases, only when the Virgin's vision for her life is found to conflict with others' plans for her does the need for a **Secret World** develop. Jas loses her freedom when her mother sees her roughhousing with boys in the park (*Bend It Like Beckham*). Subsequently, the family denies her the freedom to play soccer and insists she focus her attention on cooking a full Indian dinner. Here, the **Dependent World** is afraid of the Virgin exploring her independent spirit. They try to get control of her before she has too much power for them to be able to assert their will, as happened with Jas's cousin who is now a fashion designer divorced from a white boy with blue hair.

The separation of the **Secret World** and the **Dependent World** can simply be a state of mind. In *Pretty Woman*, Vivian sees herself as a service provider to her client, Edward, until she kisses him on the mouth. There is a world they experience in the hotel room as well as one they experience in public, but it is their state of mind rather than the physical space that determines the **Dependent** and **Secret Worlds**.

In *New Waterford Girl*, the **Secret World** is Moonie's plan to pretend to be pregnant in order to be sent away. If this plan succeeds, Moonie can go to art school in New York City on a scholarship. Anyone who becomes a party to Moonie's plan, such as her teacher and best friend, enters her **Secret World**.

The Virgin is drawn back to the **Secret World** by positive reinforcement from the love interest. The gift of beauty, as in being true to your soul, can be receiving love, which encourages the Virgin along her path towards her dream. The Prince/Hero will often pass over many girls, declaring them silly although they are outwardly beautiful, before he is struck by the special quality in the Virgin. *Bridget Jones's Diary, Ella Enchanted, Me and the Prince,* and *Ever After* all demonstrate this point.

FEAR OF DISCOVERY

One of the key elements of the **Secret World** is the fear of discovery as the Virgin moves back and forth between the worlds. There is a constant tension that the Virgin will be exposed before she is strong enough to stand on her own. Sometimes the Virgin simply recognizes she has gained something she highly values in her **Secret World** and fears losing it, as in *While You Were Sleeping,* where Lucy clings to the feeling of having a family, and in *Wedding Crashers,* where John wants more than anything to be genuine with Claire.

Alternatively, the Virgin may fear mortal danger if she is discovered in her **Secret World**. In *Ever After,* Danielle suffers low social status and is subject to whatever cruelty her stepmother vents upon her if she is discovered meeting the Prince. The Prince thinks Danielle is a courtier and she is unsure what his reaction will be when he discovers she is a servant girl since it is illegal to impersonate someone above her station in life. In *Shakespeare in Love,* Viola's father stands to gain his greatest dream of social respectability if Viola is compliant and marries a count. Her father legally owns Viola and can inflict pain if she jeopardizes her marriageability. Furthermore, under the law of the time women who acted in the theater could be imprisoned. In *Brokeback Mountain,* Ennis has a graphic memory of the brutal murder of a homosexual man, which haunts him as he moves back and forth between his **Secret World** of passion with Jack and his **Dependent World** where he struggles to be a good husband and father. Ennis curses the day he met Jack.

Sometimes the fear may be of a metaphoric death, such as the loss of love, the loss of a dream, or the loss of a job. In *Bend It Like Beckham*, Jas risks causing her family emotional pain if she is not compliant with their wishes. She is strongly attached to her family and questions whether she has the right to inflict so much pain on them to satisfy her dream. In *She's the Man*, Viola has dreamed of playing college soccer all her life. If they discover she is a girl on the men's team, she will be socially disgraced and lose her last opportunity to show her community that she can be a soccer star.

The fear of being discovered in the **Secret World** can also be portrayed in a comic way as the Virgin slips from one world to the other, changing outfits, forgetting that she is still wearing the sideburns of a boy (*Shakespeare in Love* and *She's the Man*) or slipping from one room to another and trying to provide a reasonable explanation to the bystander. Lucy, in *While You Were Sleeping*, is hilarious as she cleverly pulls together bits of information to keep the family believing she is Peter's fiancée.

However the Virgin finds her **Secret World**, it is there that she experiments, practices, and grows toward realizing her dream for herself.

Stage Six: No Longer Fits Her World

Through spending time in her **Secret World**, the Virgin increases her power in the form of self-knowledge, and starts to see her dream as a possible reality. It is also becoming clear to the Virgin that she cannot juggle these two worlds forever. She is defining her own values and claiming her personal authority. There is a growing discomfort with going back to the **Dependent World** and angst about having a **Secret World**.

There are several changes in the Virgin's behavior that indicate she **No Longer Fits Her Dependent** or **Secret World**. She may become reckless, become confused, attract attention, or declare the task too hard.

Becomes Reckless

The Virgin lowers her protective barriers as she develops her passion, sometimes becoming reckless. In *Wedding Crashers*, John breaks the rules of wedding crashing and becomes emotionally involved with Claire. He and Jeremy stay too long in their **Secret World** despite all the warning signs. When Claire directly asks if John is a wedding crasher, he answers "Yes, with shades of gray." The old John would have come up with a really good lie to answer her question. No longer comfortable in his old style, he tells the truth, which ironically makes him look sleazy.

Vivian breaks the rules that protect her when she kisses Edward on the mouth in *Pretty Woman*. Deloris (*Sister Act*) gets so wrapped up in helping the nuns that she allows herself to appear on television, forgetting that her ex-boyfriend has a contract out on her. These Virgins have blown their protective cover by breaking the prescribed rules of their **Secret World**.

Becomes Confused

The Virgin may also become confused as she nears her goal. As the dream takes shape she starts to think about what she is losing and becomes ambivalent about what is most important. In *New Waterford Girl*, Moonie suddenly sees the value of belonging in her small town and in her family. She misses being called Moonie by her mother, who now calls her by her Christian name. She starts to question the cost against the gain of art school.

Viola becomes confused about what she can get from Shakespeare, in *Shakespeare in Love*. She allows her anger at discovering Shakespeare is married to sabotage her dream of experiencing passion as a woman and the thrill of being an actor on stage. Viola forgets that whether he's married or not, she will never be Shakespeare's wife.

Attracts Attention

The Virgin may also attract attention as she shines, making it hard to keep her secret. Tuan described beauty as the "emotional-aspirational core of a culture – both its drive and its goal" (2). Seeing the soul of a person in turn stirs the soul of the seer.

Fear of being discovered becomes more legitimate as the Virgin grows towards her dream; she inspires others. The ripple effect draws attention back to the source. In *Ever After* and *While You Were Sleeping,* the male lead is inspired towards his dream as he experiences the inspiration of the Virgin. People want to know what has caused the change in him and this points attention back to the Virgin.

Declares the Task Too Hard

Another way the Virgin **No Longer Fits Her World** is when she feels the task before her is just too hard and she is tempted to slip back to her **Dependent World**. In *Miss Congeniality,* Grace has been challenged to face her attitudes towards her femininity and acknowledge how lonely her life is when all she wants to do is stop a murder. She pulls a gun on her trainer to get a donut and tells Eric she quits.

In *Legally Blond,* when Elle's boss/professor makes a pass at her, she quits her job and is ready to quit law school. She takes on the views of her parents once again when she says, "All people ever see is blond hair and boobs. I was just kidding myself. It turns out I am a joke." Elle is declaring the task too hard.

Billy starts to recognize that his dream is growing and that it is going to be harder than he imagined (*Billy Elliot*). He will have to leave his hometown and his brother, father, and grandmother, and live alone in a big city. Billy tries to sabotage his relationship with his dance instructor rather than take the step of auditioning for dance school.

The Virgin keeps coming back to her **Secret World** and fights to retain the private space of this cocoon. However, reckless or confused behavior may trigger a warning shot in the Virgin's direction. There may be some form of retribution for her lack of conformity. In *Ever After,* the stepsister burns the book *Utopia* that Danielle's father gave her shortly before he died. Her stepmother confiscates the dress and shoes left to Danielle by her mother. Ennis is accused of being homosexual by his wife, causing him to resort to violence to protect his secret in *Brokeback Mountain*. Narrowly, the Virgin manages to keep her **Secret World** but she is graphically aware of the dangerous game she is playing.

Stage Seven: Caught Shining

At this point in the archetypal structure, reality hits and the Virgin must face the fact that she cannot keep her two worlds separated anymore. The **Secret World** and the **Dependent World** collide and the feared consequences manifest. The Virgin often finds herself punished, shamed, or exiled.

There is a strong reaction to the discovery that the Virgin has a dream for herself and that she has taken action towards realizing that dream against the wishes of others. In *Billy Elliot,* when Billy's father sees Billy dancing with his gay friend, who is wearing a tutu, he believes he has witnessed a gay love scene. This creates a public humiliation for Billy's father. It occurs in the boxing ring, not the dance studio, which highlights the femininity of their actions by the juxtaposition and increases the insult to masculinity.

The Virgin is **Caught Shining** in several different ways. She may grow too big, find her circumstances change, be recognized by her **Dependent World** while in her **Secret World**, or be betrayed.

GROWS TOO BIG

The Virgin has spent a period growing in her cocoon. Eventually she will grow too big to be contained by the **Secret World,** which exists within the **Dependent World.** In *Brokeback Mountain,* when Jack takes more chances to be true to his sexual nature by rendezvousing with a man at a friend's cabin, he pays the price with his brutal murder. His **Dependent** and **Secret Worlds** collide. Ennis is left to live with this lesson.

When *Tootsie* becomes ragingly popular with female audiences, Michael Dorsey is unable to express his love to a woman who thinks he is a woman (and whose father has proposed marriage to him). Michael also can't get acting roles as a man when he is believed to be a woman. The success he finds in his **Secret World** has become the block to his dream of being recognized as an actor and a man.

CIRCUMSTANCES CHANGE

The two worlds may collide when the circumstances that created the **Secret World** change. When Tess's boss comes back early in *Working Girl,* Tess is exposed as a secretary posing as an entrepreneur at a crucial meeting. She is shamed for being deceitful and is forced to leave the meeting.

When Peter comes out of his coma in *While You Were Sleeping,* he doesn't recognize Lucy. Lucy is caught in her lie that she is Peter's fiancée.

RECOGNIZED BY HER DEPENDENT WORLD

Another way the Virgin is **Caught Shining** is when someone in her **Secret World** recognizes her from her **Dependent World.** In *The Sound of Music,* Maria cannot hide her feelings for the Captain when she dances with him. The Baroness recognizes that Maria is in love with her fiancé and sends Maria back to the convent.

In *Maid in Manhattan,* Marisa is recognized by a hotel guest as an employee fraternizing with the guests. Hotel security tapes show her leaving Chris's room in the early hours. Further investigation shows Marisa wearing a Dolce suit belonging to a guest. Marisa and a fellow employee lose their jobs and Marisa is publicly shamed.

BETRAYED

The two worlds of the Virgin may collide because she is counting on someone and that person betrays her. Danielle (*Ever After*) is publicly shamed at the ball when her stepmother rips off her costume wings and identifies Danielle as her servant. The Prince turns his back on Danielle, unable to overcome the news of her humble status. Danielle is then sold to a Lecher and exiled from her childhood home.

Viola is betrayed by a disgruntled fellow actor who puts a mouse in her shirt to force her to expose herself as a woman on the stage, in *Shakespeare in Love.* In *Strictly Ballroom,* Scott is betrayed by false information concerning his father to get him to comply with the wishes of his dance school. Scott in turn betrays Fran and agrees to dance competitively with another woman.

In **Caught Shining** the dream of the Virgin is no longer a secret. She is revealed to the world.

Stage Eight: Gives Up What Kept Her Stuck

Just as a butterfly sheds a drop of blood as it emerges from its cocoon and experiences a period of vulnerability, the Virgin must sacrifice some of her past to move into her future. **Gives Up What Kept Her Stuck** is the major turning point in the psychological growth of the Virgin. It is also one of the most difficult to clearly express and the key to the deeper meaning in the story. It identifies the dialogue in the Virgin's head that has kept her from moving forward and realizing her dream. In psychological terms, she is overcoming the complex that has been holding her back.

In the **Price of Conformity**, the Virgin had an experience that developed into a complex, burying her pain in her personal unconscious and creating a belief or a pattern of behavior that keeps her from taking action and claiming her life. In **Gives Up What Kept Her Stuck**, she brings that belief or behavior to her conscious level and challenges it. She asks the direct question, testing whether her belief or behavior will really get her what she hoped, or if she still wants what it was giving her. She decides that the complex is no longer serving her well. This belief or behavior made sense when she had limited resources, but it is incompatible with her current desire to be her own person. She has lost her dream life and must take the steps necessary to make it her reality. That process begins with letting something go, allowing it to die. As with all kinds of death, it is not an easy stage of life and there will be grief and sometimes harsh realities to face.

The main drive for the Virgin to stay stuck is a belief that conformity to the **Dependent World** is required to secure safety, or to maintain or earn love. When what has kept her stuck concerns love, the Virgin questions the belief that she is loved unconditionally and is prepared to accept the answer either way. When it concerns safety, the Virgin gives up the belief that she is unable to take care of herself. **Gives Up What Kept Her Stuck** frees the activation energy that allows the Virgin to complete her quest to achieve her dream.

This moment of recognition is often marked symbolically by the tolling of a bell, an alarm sounding, or a strike of lightning. There can be a loss of faith, a loss of a relationship or an imminent death that is a metaphor for the death that must occur (Woodman, 27).

FEAR OF BEING HURT

The fear of being hurt is a common complex the Virgin holds. In *About a Boy,* Will recognizes that he no longer wants to be an island. He has isolated himself in order to feel protected from the humiliation he experienced as a child. Will's **Price of Conformity** was to perform his father's tacky Christmas jingle in front of his parents' friends and watch his father's humiliation at being a one-hit-wonder. Becoming an island was a perfect defense for Will as a child. The problem is, Will is no longer a child and the defense is preventing him from becoming an adult and entering into relationships or taking risks and fulfilling his dream of making music. Will wants to be important to someone and to have meaning in his life. From his depression, he realizes that he needs to care about someone and that someone is Marcus, so Will decides to get involved in the mess of Marcus's life.

Gracie Hart, in *Miss Congeniality,* experienced rejection from boys as a child, so she developed a complex where she rejects her femininity. Gracie's **Price of Conformity** is to have a masculine demeanor and a belief that feminine women are stupid and empty. This belief is leaving her unfulfilled as a woman, lonely and out of balance. In **Gives Up What Kept Her Stuck,** Gracie acknowledges that the beauty pageant contestants are intelligent, kind and beautiful people, worthy of her protection, and she wishes to have their feminine qualities. This frees Gracie to have a relationship with her feminine self and receive Eric's romantic attention.

Envy also causes the Virgin to believe she needs to make herself small so she doesn't invoke the wrath of others (Ulanov, 27). In *Pretty Woman,* Vivian grew up with her mother telling her she was no good and only worthy of "bums." She needs to stop this message from running in her head before she can respect herself and expect respect from others.

In *Working Girl,* Tess waits until the last minute to speak up for herself. Finally, she ignores the warning, cleverly planted in the **Price of Conformity,** that if she doesn't get along with people, she will be unemployable. Tess blows the business deal wide open, while at the same time putting her boss Catherine as well as the potential investor, Mr. Trask, in turmoil. She decides to do what is honest and right for her, regardless of who it inconveniences. No more will she be a mousy nice-girl.

Fear of danger sends Sleeping Beauty into an isolated world peopled only by fairies and animals. Sleeping Beauty must stop believing the tales people are telling her about her life and join the world. In the cautionary tale *The Virgin Suicides*, Lux takes a chance and allows Trip into her life but he lets her down. She allows Trip into her life and he lets her down. In this tragic failed Virgin story, Lux fails to recognize that her mother is a danger to her and that she has the power to stop conforming to her mother's rules. This failure to give up her controlling belief leads to her depression and suicide.

Gives Up What Kept Her Stuck in *Virgin Suicides*

Scott listens to what his mother and his dance club wants of him in *Strictly Ballroom*, and, in choosing to conform, he learns that he is a fool. Club members pressure him to dance the conventional dance steps to gain the glory of winning. He conforms only to learn that the contest winner was determined before he stepped onto the floor. He sold out himself and his partner Fran for the belief that approval from the Dance Federation was the true measure of good dancing. When Scott gives up that belief and dances according to his own principles, he is no longer stuck.

In *Brokeback Mountain*, Ennis hid his homosexual feelings by marrying a woman, and after the divorce, dating women. Ennis finally gives up believing he can force himself to be what he is not and stops dating.

FEAR OF LOSS OF LOVE

Cinderella needs to stop endlessly serving others and realize she will not secure love through servitude. Sometimes the Virgin may feel loveable only when she keeps her views in alignment with her father's or the dominant views of her kingdom. This belief must change for her to realize her dream.

In *Ever After*, Danielle complies with being her stepmother's servant, with the hope that she will someday know the love of a mother. After the fiasco at the ball, where her stepmother exposes and humiliates her, Danielle asks her stepmother if she has ever loved her. The stepmother reveals Danielle was never more than a pebble in her shoe. With a nod, Danielle accepts this painful truth. Learning this is both heartbreaking and freeing as she is now able to let go of the hope that she will ever receive love from her stepmother.

In *Shrek*, Princess Fiona has the ability to free herself from the dragon, but pretends to be asleep, convinced she must await true love's first kiss. She sublimates her feelings for Shrek and the vile nature of Lord Farquaad until the last moment, when she realizes that love's true form is that of an ogre. In that moment, Fiona gives up the belief that she is destined to marry a Prince and redefines her ideal of beauty.

In *Bend It Like Beckham*, Jas's parents are asserting their will over Jas to maintain Indian traditional values. She risks their love and respect if she defies them by continuing to follow her passion for soccer. Jas agrees to conform to the wishes of her family but refuses to pretend she is happy. She makes it clear that she does not want to lose the love of her family. Jas is rewarded for her expression of love when her father reciprocates by saying that he wants her to be happy more than he wants her to keep tradition. Jas knows she is unconditionally loved as she reaches for her dream of playing soccer. Jas gave up the belief that she had to be compliant with her father's wishes to secure love. Expressing her desires and offering to sacrifice them in favor of parental happiness was a risky move. If her family did not have unconditional love for her, Jas would eventually have had to go against their wishes to fulfill her destiny as a Virgin or risk depression and insanity.

Billy dances secretly because he fears his father will assume him to be gay and be unable to love and accept him. Billy believes that his father's love is conditional until one day Billy is caught dancing with a gay friend. In a split second Billy decides to show his father his passion for dance and to test whether his father will still love him.

Gives Up What Kept Her Stuck in *Billy Elliot*

Until this point in the Virgin's story she believed that she must be passive, servile, small, or nice. She now gives up that belief and becomes rebellious. She recognizes that she does not have to accept other people's authority over her or others' visions for her life.

Stage Nine: Kingdom in Chaos

A ripple effect takes place as the Virgin begins to change and the result is chaos in the kingdom. The world becomes uncomfortable. What was an isolated craziness as the Virgin juggled her two worlds, now affects many people. The old sense of order begins to crumble.

In *She's the Man*, the **Kingdom in Chaos** stage is where hearts are broken, identities mistaken, and the greater purpose of proving that girls can play soccer as well as boys is threatened. In *Maid in Manhattan*, good men lose their jobs and Chris faces another public scandal that threatens his election campaign. The ugly premise that it is dangerous for the lower classes to forget their place is in the public domain. In *Sister Act*, nuns are being threatened by gangsters and are seen shuffling all over Las Vegas among slot machines and lounge entertainers.

When traditions are threatened, an effort to defend the old order is launched. In *Bend It Like Beckham*, the sister's wedding is called off because Jas's behavior has reflected badly on her family. In *Bollywood/Hollywood*, Pinky's wedding is called off because her brother has deceived his mother with a false engagement. Learning Pinky is pregnant adds to the sense of chaos. Billy's father becomes a scab to provide for Billy's dancing lessons and goes against the severe traditions of union workers, giving up his place in the community, to support his son (*Billy Elliot*).

Often the chaos in the kingdom has no direct connection to the Virgin. Her awakening has merely stirred the winds of change to create synchronicities. In *Billy Elliot*, Billy's brother is chased through the neighbor's homes by the police and is arrested, and the family is thrown further apart. In *New Waterford Girl*, a pregnant unwed girl returns and proudly announces she is going to have her baby in the Catholic town.

During the **Kingdom in Chaos** stage, there is a reaction to the Virgin asserting decision-making power over her life. But, as the Kingdom knows, it is not too late to go back and restore the old order. The Kingdom uses all its power to bring the Virgin back in line.

Stage Ten: Wanders in the Wilderness

It is one thing for the Virgin to follow her dream in the **Secret World** while the **Dependent World** still exists for her as a fall-back position. It is very different to stand up to the **Dependent World** and follow her dream whatever the consequences.

The Virgin has gone against her **Dependent World** and is unsure of her ability to stand alone. There is no guarantee that she can make it on her own. She is at a fork in the road: go back and appease the **Dependent World**, which seems the easiest option because it keeps most people happy, or go forward and make a new place for herself.

Tess (*Working Girl*) has no home, no job, and a lousy reputation in the business world. Her old boyfriend is engaged but there is still a glimmer in his eye for Tess. If he marries someone else, Tess will also lose her tenuous place with the old high-school gang. She already has a new appearance and aspirations.

The Virgin may find that she is vulnerable without her **Dependent World**. In *Sister Act*, Deloris wants to lead the nuns in singing for the Pope but her old life catches up with her. Gangsters kidnap her and the only thing keeping her alive is the possibility that her nun's habit is more than a costume. With a gun to her head, Deloris is unsure of whether the nuns will stand by her because she has deceived them, pretending to be a nun when she is really a lounge singer.

In *Pretty Woman*, Vivian has gained enough self-esteem to stop turning tricks on the street, but will she allow herself to be Edward's call girl? Will she accept his offer to be kept in an apartment or will she believe in herself and wait for a relationship that comes with respect?

The **Wanders in the Wilderness** stage is a test of the Virgin's conviction and it is her moment of doubt. She is faced with an opportunity to demonstrate her growth and no longer accept a world that requires her to be smaller than she can be. In *Bollywood/Hollywood*, Sue is accosted by a drunk and Rahul defends her, but he does so to silence the drunk. Sue recognizes that he has defended her for the wrong reason: male pride rather than a belief in her. Rahul is like her father, thinking only of how a situation affects him. Sue loves Rahul and his family, and knows she will be well cared for if she marries him, but will Sue enter into another diminishing relationship for the trade-off of safety?

Billy's choice to dance caused family upheaval but they proved their unconditional love for him. Now he must decide whether he has the strength to face the world alone, including assumptions that he is gay. At the tryouts, a boy makes a pass at him and Billy resorts to violence, jeopardizing his dream (*Billy Elliot*).

Wanders in the Wilderness is the second stage of changing beliefs, and in it, life is uncomfortable. The Virgin must emotionally separate from the world she has known and feel the essence of being alone. Her choice to move towards change in the face of hardship is the mark of a strong character and the indication that change will stand the test of time.

Stage Eleven: Chooses Her Light

In **Chooses Her Light**, the Virgin decides to trust herself and pursue her dream or passion, whatever happens. This is the last stage of her transformation and a joyous climax to her story. She would rather shine than be safe or maintain order.

In *About a Boy*, Will joins Marcus onstage, no longer alone, even if they are fools together. Billy discards his protective shell and expresses his feelings when he dances, earning him a place in dance school (*Billy Elliot*). In *While You Were Sleeping*, Lucy is at the altar, about to marry Peter, when she chooses to wait for true love and confesses her love for Jack. In *Pretty Woman*, Vivian refuses Edward's generous offer to keep her in an apartment because what she really wants is a committed, respectful relationship. Ennis decides he will go to his daughter's wedding and society will just have to deal with it (*Brokeback Mountain*). Through these actions all the Virgins choose a path for themselves.

Chooses Her Light in *About a Boy*

In **Chooses Her Light**, the Virgin introduces her true form to her kingdom. She goes to the ball and is radiantly beautiful before her entire kingdom in a lovely metaphor for her true nature shining in a public way. It is the profound act of coming out. It is fun, exciting and often magical, because the Virgin is finally ready to be seen as her true self.

The choice the Virgin makes when she **Chooses Her Light** is a clear action towards her dream. She applies for the job (*Maid in Manhattan*), competes for a place on the figure skating team (*Ice Princess*), or challenges the ruling class (*Ever After*). Some tangible, finite goal is reached. This is the third and final stage of changing a belief. It is important that the decision to pursue her dream and be true to herself is an identifiable action made by the Virgin.

In some cases, after the Virgin chooses her dream, her action precipitates danger and she is rescued. Never does she need to be rescued, then choose to love her rescuer as fulfillment of the **Chooses Her Light** beat. This would be a major step backwards into another **Dependent World**.

The Virgin integrates her inner desire for herself with her actions in the world, and claims her dream regardless of the consequences. In no way is she waiting to be rescued. This is the point where Scott dances new steps with Fran (*Strictly Ballroom*), John tells Claire how he feels even though he knows her boyfriend will beat him up (*Wedding Crashers*), and Viola plays a woman in Shakespeare's play even though she risks prison (*Shakespeare in Love*). It is boldly being true to herself in the face of oppressive power.

Stage Twelve: Re-Ordering (Rescue)

The Virgin has moved from secretly claiming some personal authority to being authentic in all parts of her life. The shadow side, the Whore or Victim, has been banished and the Virgin has challenged her kingdom to accept she has her own vision for her life. This is the **Re-ordering**.

A good **Re-ordering**, from the feminine perspective, has two elements: it recognizes the Virgin's true value when she is fulfilling her dream; and it reconnects the Virgin with a community.

SEES HER VALUE

Jas's father, in *Bend It Like Beckham*, stands up against his wife, his personal demons, and the teachings of his traditions to support Jas in playing soccer. When he recognizes that supporting

Jas in her dream is more important than having a compliant daughter, he affirms Jas as having value to him beyond her contribution to the stability of his values. He changes his conditional love to a love that accepts her personal authority and to follow her dream of playing soccer in America.

In *Ever After*, Danielle saves herself from physical harm but she still has no kingdom in which to exist in her new, shining state. It is when Prince Henry arrives and admits he has failed Danielle, vowing to love her as a peasant or a queen, that the **Re-ordering** is complete. When Prince Henry changes his values to see the real person, as opposed to her station in life, he is affirming the value of Danielle and the teachings of *Utopia* that she has brought to life for him. Danielle is released from a flawed kingdom and a new one is created.

In *Working Girl*, Jack plays the Hero when he stands up for Tess, against her boss who is his lover, placing his own career in jeopardy. He does not do this because Tess is beautiful or to demonstrate his strength. Jack speaks up for Tess because he knows she is a worthy business partner.

RECONNECTS HER WITH THE KINGDOM

The obstacle, established in the **Dependent World**, that kept the Virgin from living her dream, must be addressed in the **Re-ordering**. Family unity, the continuation of traditional values, the secure transfer of family fortunes, patriarchy, social values, religious traditions, or conditional love have been threatened by the actions of the Virgin.

The Virgin has brought chaos to the kingdom and now it is time to put the kingdom back together again. This may happen through love, where the Tyrant grows into the Lover/King. Alternatively, the actions of the Hero may eliminate the evil force, to the benefit of all.

It is not necessary for the shining Virgin's community to be the whole kingdom. It could be a few people from her kingdom who support her. In *Brokeback Mountain,* the reconnection of the Virgin with the kingdom occurs when Ennis's daughter, Alma, asks Ennis to come to her wedding. Alma is asking him to join her in her world after standing by Ennis all through her childhood. Alma re-orders Ennis's world by giving him a place of honor as her highly loved father. The moment does not have to be full of action to be powerful. It must, however, satisfy the need to value the Virgin in her true form and reconnect the Virgin to a community.

Other times the oppressive force is not interested in growing and must be eliminated. This is when the **Re-ordering** is also known as the **Rescue**. It is not the nature of the Virgin to assert her will over the will of others. She inspires others to change out of love or a drive towards joy. The Hero, on the other hand, does assert his will against evil. When the **Dependent World** of the Virgin includes an oppressive force that the kingdom needs to be free of, the Hero takes on the task of eliminating it, inspired by the Virgin. Here the journeys of the Virgin and the Hero overlap and support each other.

The kingdom is challenged to accommodate the authentic Virgin and this creates resistance. The chaos brought about by the Virgin's claiming her personal authority can cause the facade to crumble from the evil element of society, exposing it to the kingdom. Love for the Virgin inspires the people, or a Hero, to stand up to the exposed evil element. This evil element is not willing to go quietly and identifies the Virgin as the source of its problem, placing her in real danger. Examples of movies where the threat of patriarchal dominance has been removed include *Wedding Crashers, Sister Act,* and *Dirty Dancing.* In *Wedding Crashers,* Claire is free of her domineering boyfriend and John and Jason have overcome their fear of intimacy. Deloris's boyfriend is neutralized and forced to pay for his crimes (*Sister Act*), and nobody puts Baby in the corner anymore (*Dirty Dancing*).

THE FALSE RESCUE

The feminine perspective of what is seminal in the **Rescue** is quite different from the Hero's perspective. The **Rescue** must recognize the true value of the Virgin and reconnect the Virgin with her community. A **False Rescue** is when the Hero fights for the Virgin, but only to prove he is brave or to assert his will over another, not because he sees the value of the Virgin. Examples of the false rescue are found in movies like *Pretty Woman* and *Bollywood/Hollywood*. The reasons behind the Hero's actions are crucial to the Virgin's future. If he is "saving" the Virgin for any reason other than in recognition of her value and to reconnect her to her kingdom, it is potentially a new **Dependent World**. Ultimately, this is a test of the Virgin and is linked to **Wanders in the Wilderness**. Will she enter into another **Dependent World** or has she learned the lesson of her journey?

In *Pretty Woman*, after Vivian learns to value herself and believe in her talent, Edward offers to keep her in an apartment, safe from the streets. When Edward's friend and business partner attempts to rape Vivian, Edward appears very heroic, punching his partner in the nose and ending their partnership. However, he still wants to keep Vivian as his hooker. He is only offering

The False Rescue in *Pretty Woman*

to make her a safe hooker. Edward does not recognize the value of the Virgin or the fact that she must have a new kingdom in which to exist in her shining form. Vivian sees that Edward has failed the test and accepts the result by leaving him. Eventually, Edward realizes he has made a mistake and the true **Rescue** occurs when he conquers his fear of heights (a metaphor for commitment) and climbs the staircase to offer Vivian his respect and commitment.

The **False Rescue** is really offering the Virgin a chance to go back to the **Dependent World**. She is offered comfort, privilege, or safety. All these deprive her of the knowledge that she can count on herself and make choices in the world. She will never be able to love unconditionally if she does not understand her power and learn that she can stand on her own.

THE TEST

The **Re-ordering (Rescue)** affirms the Virgin's growth. When the Hero fails to value her true nature she must reject him. In the beginning, the Virgin was dependent on the world into which she was born. Now she has a choice of where she places her trust and what she calls her kingdom. The **Re-ordering (Rescue)** demonstrates that the Virgin is wiser now and will not allow others to dominate her.

As a test, the Rescue provides the Obstacle to Love crucial to writing a compelling romance. The Obstacle to Love in a Virgin story is when the Hero fails to value the Virgin in her authentic form due to his immaturity (*Ever After*), fear of commitment (*Pretty Woman*), fear of embarrassment (*About a Boy*), or an overvaluing of the economy-driven society (*Working Girl*).

MULTIPLE RESCUES

The **Re-ordering** can occur several times in a movie. In *New Waterford Girl* there are five forms of rescue including two false rescues, two partial rescues, and one rescue that includes the two elements of seeing the Virgin's value and adjusting the kingdom to accommodate her.

The first attempt at a rescue occurs when Moonie's plan to fake a pregnancy and go to art school is working and she is about to be sent away from her community. Then one of the boys, Joey, tells Moonie's dad that none of the boys accused of impregnating Moonie has done the deed. Joey is willing to admit he didn't have sex because he believes he is saving Moonie by preserving her reputation and keeping her in their small town. This **False Rescue** is well-intentioned but a prison for Moonie. Moonie's father then tries to rescue Moonie by identifying another possible person responsible for impregnating his daughter – her teacher. Moonie's father goes after the teacher, attempting a shotgun wedding. Like Joey, the father thinks he is doing the right thing but he is really preserving the community in its current values and foiling the Virgin's efforts to shine.

Then Moonie's father does a very surprising thing. He bakes a fabulous chocolate cake, invites the neighbors over to share it, and offers a piece to Moonie. Rather than shaming his daughter to punish her, he offers her sweets at the family table, with the neighbors. It is a lovely moment of unconditional love. He doesn't agree with what he thinks she has done, but he is going to love her anyway and give her community. This is a half **Re-ordering** because Moonie still needs to be valued as an artist, but she is reconnected to her kingdom.

The teacher decides to throw away his teaching reputation, the one thing he still has going for him, and pretend to be guilty of impregnating Moonie so she can go to art school. This is another half **Re-ordering**. He is laying down his life for her but he is not reconnecting Moonie to her kingdom.

The mother is the most interesting rescuer of them all. At what point does she recognize that her daughter has created an elaborate plan so she can go to school in New York? Is it before or after she destroys the teacher's trailer? When she rams the trailer over the cliff, it might be because she sees that the teacher is trying to save Moonie. She decides that if the teacher is going to be the man in her daughter's life, he has to stop this self-pitying life in a trailer and get out there and make himself worthy. When the mom gives Moonie the note, saying she knows Moonie is faking pregnancy to go to art school and she supports her and will smooth it out with the community, the **Re-ordering** is complete.

Stage Thirteen: The Kingdom Is Brighter

The Virgin has challenged the kingdom and thrown it into chaos. They have accepted her back and made adjustments to accommodate her authentic nature or her dream. When the dust settles, the kingdom comes to realize that it is better off for having gone through this experience with the Virgin, for it was in need of change. In some way it has adjusted itself and benefited. The most common benefits include that evil has been revealed and removed, new life has been injected into the kingdom, others are inspired to follow their dreams, and unconditional love binds the kingdom.

EVIL HAS BEEN UNCOVERED AND REMOVED

Often envy or patriarchal dominance is the evil force that has been removed. An envious stepsister may come to see the Virgin as a person as opposed to a target to be shot down (*What a Girl Wants*). Reconnecting with love removes the destructive energy and energizes the kingdom.

Alternatively, the Virgin's journey may have exposed the true nature of the stepmother and she is removed by the kingdom. In *Ever After*, the stepmother has been reduced to servant status where her efforts to assert her power for her own benefit are merely laughable. We also see Danielle comfortable among the ruling class, hinting that the principles of *Utopia* will be the new style of ruling in the land.

NEW LIFE HAS BEEN INJECTED INTO THE KINGDOM

What was good for the Virgin is good for the kingdom, similar to the goose and the gander. When the Virgin realizes her dream, others are inspired to do the same. Tess broke through the glass ceiling in *Working Girl* and became a junior account executive. Now she has her own secretary and a chance to redefine the executive-secretary relationship. She mentors her secretary to do the same thing she has done. A similar scenario occurs in *Maid in Manhattan*, where Marisa works her way up from chambermaid to management and brings several of her co-workers with her. The kingdom has rethought its class structure and made space for hard-working, talented people of any rank or background to move up.

In *Sister Act* Deloris puts out a series of spiritual albums with the nuns and the church experiences a revitalization. Through a montage of album covers and the cover of *Rolling Stone*, we are left with the warm sense that change is good. The new dance steps in *Strictly Ballroom* revitalize the dance world and heal a

The Kingdom is Brighter in *Sister Act*

long-standing rift between Scott's dad and mom. Elle challenges Aristotle's concept that the law is reason without emotion, and encourages her graduating class to practice law guided by their values and passions (*Legally Blond*). In *Billy Elliot* the once homophobic father and brother sit next to Billy's childhood friend, who is in drag with his boyfriend, and together they beam with pride at Billy's achievement and experience the wonder of art. Their common love for Billy has created a new tolerance.

In all these movies, the message is that shaking up the old order has added some new life to the kingdom, and it has found a new point of equilibrium. Often this is expressed through a montage or a series of stills with a caption that gives us a look at the future and how the Kingdom has blossomed through knowing the Virgin.

UNCONDITIONAL LOVE BINDS THE KINGDOM

When the Virgin is loved for who she believes herself to be, rather than because she is meeting the expectations of others, she has moved from knowing conditional love to unconditional love. This type of love creates a strong and meaningful bond between the Virgin and the kingdom. Unconditional love then spreads to other members of the kingdom.

In *About a Boy*, Will is able to be himself and lounge on the couch in the company of a collection of loving people. His running shoes may miss the mark of being cool but he is still lovable. Under the umbrella of Will's growth, Marcus has a backup group now and his mother has the support she needs.

While You Were Sleeping also ends with a sense of unconditional love. Despite Lucy's deceiving the family, they see her inner beauty and value, and want her in their family. Jack and Lucy's genuine love for each other keeps the family unit strong, ensuring the continued existence of the unconditional love that exists in the older generation.

When the Virgin is established in her power with her dream realized, a new sense of order is found and the kingdom is brighter. It shifted to accommodate the Virgin and found that the new boundaries created a more vibrant, more tolerant, or more creative kingdom.

Virgin Film Summaries

The following film capsules look at the archetypal beats of entire Virgin movies to show how well the beats summarize the key points of a story. The film capsules also show how beats can be used in different order or repeated. The numbers in brackets indicate the stages of the Virgin story as described above.

About a Boy

Will lives off an inheritance from his father's one-hit wonder. He lives as an island, free of all risk of being embarrassed by things like trying to be a songwriter/singer (1). Yet, he is alone, always ending up the schmuck in relationships, putting up walls and being a blank (2). One day he discovers that single moms want sex but no commitment. By comparison to their ex-husbands, he is a god (3). So he gets a toddler car seat and joins a single parents club to meet single moms (4). Will meets a mom and a boy named Marcus whose mother, Fiona, has a suicidal episode. Marcus reaches out to Will to give him a safety net and they develop an unlikely connection as Will teaches Marcus how to be cool (5). At a New Year's party, Will meets a single mom named Rachael and insinuates that Marcus is his son because it gives Will and Rachael common ground (5). Will's world stops making sense to him because he cares about Rachael and wants to be worthy of her (6). Will tells Rachael that Marcus is not his son and loses Rachael (7). Will rejects Marcus just as Fiona lapses back into a suicidal depression (9). Desperate, Marcus decides to perform *Killing Me Softly* at the school rock concert to please his mom, which is social suicide for Marcus (9). Will goes into a depression (10). As Will hits bottom he realizes he is no longer willing to be an island because if he doesn't care about anyone or anything, no one will care about him (8). Will cares about Marcus and decides to get involved in Marcus's life (11). Will goes to Fiona and says he wants to help. Fiona appreciates the gesture but doesn't feel suicidal at the moment. She asks Will to take her to the school concert to see Marcus perform. Will freaks and speeds to the school. Unable to talk Marcus out of performing, Will joins him on stage where they are so outrageously embarrassing they are a hit (12). Then, Will closes his eyes and sings, snubbing his greatest fear of ridicule, as the audience throws tomatoes (11). Rachael is in the audience and sees Will is not a blank. By Christmas, Will, Marcus and Fiona have back-up people who care about them (13).

About a Boy scores thirteen out of thirteen.

Angels in the Outfield

Rodger lives in temporary foster care with his friend JP (1). Rodger's father is about to legally give Rodger up (2). Rodger wants them to be a family more than anything but his father says that is as likely as the Angels winning the pennant. So Rodger prays to the stars that the Angels will win (3). Real angels start showing up at the games to help the Angel players but only Rodger can see them (5). Coach Knox makes Rodger and PJ honorary mascots with ball caps and jackets (4), hoping to keep the winning streak going. Rodger's belief in the team spreads to the coach, and before long, the team is playing well, sometimes without angels (5). Rodger has to keep the angels a secret because they don't like attention (5). When Ranch Wilder, the announcer, finds out Coach Knox believes in angels, it's scandal in the papers (7). Coach Knox is called upon to renounce angels and his belief in Rodger (10) or lose his career. At the same time, Rodger is legally given to the state by his father and they will never be a family (6). Coach Knox decides he would rather stand behind Rodger and the players decide to stand behind Coach Knox (12). Knox is confirmed as the coach and they take on the Red Sox for the pennant. But the angels can't help in a final game and the Angel players are on their own (6). The angels also tell Rodger the pitcher will soon develop cancer and die (9). Rodger decides believing in each other is all that is needed and he convinces the pitcher he can win the game (11). Knox believes in his players and they gel as a team (11). The Angels win the pennant, and the pitcher ends his career on a high note (13). Rodger and JP accept Coach Knox as their adoptive father and they all believe good things can happen (13).

Angels in the Outfield scores 12 out of 13. There is no clear moment where Rodger gives up his belief that his birth father will step up to the plate and be a father (8). Rodger has to let this dream go to make room for his adoptive father. Therefore, it is only implied when Rodger accepts Coach Knox as his new father that he has given up on his dream of being a family with his birth father.

Bend It Like Beckham

Jas is a teenager in a traditional Indian family, living in London (1). Her family is pulled between London norms and traditional Indian attitudes towards girls' modesty and training (1). They have a rich tradition of marriage into which Jas's sister is about to enter (1). Jas has a passion for soccer but her family insists she be nice and behave like a proper Indian woman (2). While Jas plays soccer in the park, a young soccer player named Jules sees her talent and gets Jas to try out for an organized women's soccer league (3). Jas won't wear the team soccer shorts because she has burn scars. Her coach, Joe, tells her to stop hiding and be grateful for her soccer talent (4). Jas tells Joe that her parents support her, and tells her parents she has a summer job in order to play soccer in the women's league (5). Several times her parents catch her playing soccer and each time she lies to them and plays more soccer (5). Jas's sister's wedding is called off because Jas is mistaken for kissing a boy at the bus stop (9). Secretly at a tournament in Germany, Jas almost kisses Joe and develops a rivalry with Jules over Joe. Jas never feels right lying to her parents but she knows she can't give up her passion for soccer to please them (6). The wedding is back on when the family realizes they were mistaken, but Jas's father catches Jas being racially mistreated at a soccer game and refuses to speak to her, so she conforms to his wishes (anti-11). The wedding conflicts with the final soccer tournament where a U.S. scout is coming to see Jas and Jules. Jas has lost her best friend and the respect of her father and is unable to attend the final game (10). Joe talks to Jas's father to inform him Jas has a great soccer opportunity the next day (12). Jas attends her sister's wedding but won't pretend to be happy (anti-11, 8). Jas's father tells her to go to the game and come back with a smile on her face (12). Jas plays her best game and wins the scholarship (11). Jas's gay friend announces a fake engagement under the condition that Jas can accept a U.S. soccer scholarship (half 12). Jas decides she is done with lying (8). She tells her family she is not engaged but has an opportunity to go to an American university and play women's soccer (11). Her father decides he wants Jas to stand up to racism rather than accept a bad situation as he has done (12, 13). Jas tells Joe she can accept the scholarship and Joe tries to kiss her. Jas says no (anti-11). Her family has had a lot to deal with and Jas isn't going to have secrets from them any more (11). At the airport Jas and Joe kiss good-bye and decide to openly face Jas's family at Christmas (11). Jules and Jas's families make a cross-cultural friendship and Joe plays cricket with Jas's father (13).

Bend It Like Beckham scores thirteen out of thirteen.

Billy Elliot

Billy lives with his father, brother, and grandmother in a mining town in a small company house. He cares for his grandmother, having recently lost his mother (1). His father, a miner from a long line of miners, signs Billy up for boxing lessons, where Billy gets pummeled (2). When asked to give the keys to the ballet instructor after boxing, Billy is fascinated by the dancing (3). He tries on his first pair of ballet slippers and attends a class (4). Billy uses his boxing money to take ballet lessons, practicing in the bathroom, avoiding his family's suspicions (5). People start to question Billy's sexuality (6). Billy's ballet instructor thinks Billy should apply to the Royal Ballet Academy (3). When Billy's father catches Billy dancing with his homosexual friend (7), Billy defiantly gives his dad a demonstration of his talent (8). Billy's dad runs from Billy (10). Billy, in turn, lashes out against his instructor, who is pushing him to follow his dream (10). Meanwhile, the brother is arrested and Billy misses his try-out for the Royal Ballet Academy (9). But Billy's dad, inspired by the memory of his wife, recognizes Billy deserves a chance to follow his passion, and crosses the picket line to support him (12). Unable to go through with crossing the picket line, they sell Billy's mother's jewelry to get the money for Billy to try out in London (12). Billy almost blows his chance by hitting a fellow dancer who tries to be "friendly" in the change room (10), but Billy finally stands up and describes how he feels when he dances, and is accepted into the academy (11). The son of a miner has become a famous dancer and the father and brother are exposed to a more tolerant and artistic world (13).

Billy Elliot scores thirteen out of thirteen.

Bollywood/Hollywood

Sue is living at home with her traditional East Indian family (1). She is offered to a wrestler in a traditional arranged marriage that will benefit her father (1). Angered at being sold like chattel,

Sue becomes an escort to get back at her dad (2). One night in a bar, Sue meets Rahul (3). He is stuck between the modern world and traditional Indian values. He wants to honor his father but also wants to marry for love (2). Now his mother won't allow his sister to marry until Rahul is engaged. Rahul offers Sue money to pretend to be his fiancée so Rahul's sister can get married (3). Sue accepts and goes shopping for beautiful traditional Indian dresses (4). She's a big hit at the pre-wedding party (5) because she has a gift for celebrating traditional values, blending in modern practices, and maintaining her individuality. Sue admits to Rahul that she is falling in love with him (6). Sue is then accused of being a whore in a bar and everyone discovers she is a paid escort (7). Rahul hits the man who accuses Sue, but believes the man over Sue, and Sue realizes Rahul will always doubt her trustworthiness (10). Sue decides to leave Rahul (11). Rahul is confused, his sister has eloped, his chauffeur forgets his place and offers him advice, and his mother cries "social ruin" despite once claiming to love Sue (9). Rahul sees his mother's hypocrisy and is disgusted by it, yet can't get over his own judgment of Sue (10). His grandmother tells Rahul he is a fool and that she loves Sue (12). Sue is fed up with spending her time getting back at her dad (8) and wants to focus on her life by going to school (11). Rahul finally realizes he loves Sue unconditionally and admits to Sue she is his true love no matter what her past, and offers her marriage (12). Traditional and modern values are harmonized through the union of Sue and Rahul (13). Sue's dad and Rahul have changed and opened their hearts to Sue and, by implication, to all women (13).

Bollywood/Hollywood scores thirteen out of thirteen.

Brokeback Mountain

Ennis, an out-of-work cowboy, takes a job with Jack, watching sheep in the Brokeback Mountains for the summer (1). Orphaned at a young age, Ennis was raised by his brother until his brother married, leaving Ennis to fend for himself in a harsh masculine world where he barely speaks (2). Ennis has childhood memories of his father showing him the corpse of a brutally murdered homosexual man as a part of his education (1). On the job with Jack, one of them is supposed to sleep with the sheep but it gets late and they both bunk down in camp (3). Jack approaches Ennis, removing his clothes (4), and they have intercourse and fall in love (5). Their boss makes a surprise visit and discovers them (7). Ennis is terrified and rejects Jack (6) but, as time passes and Ennis is safely married with two daughters, Jack and Ennis secretly meet on fishing trips (5). Poor, disconnected, with the kids driving them crazy, Ennis's wife becomes suspicious and Ennis is violent towards her to keep her quiet (6). They divorce (9). Jack seeks out companionship with a man in his city and is brutally beaten to death (10). Ennis visits Jack's parents and finds his shirt that Jack kept from their summer together wrapped inside Jack's shirt, acknowledging their love was real (8). Ennis lives a secluded life with Jack's memory (11). One day Ennis's daughter visits, says she is getting married, and wants Ennis to give her away (12). Ennis finds excuses not to but then decides people are just going to have to adjust to the fact that he is going to attend the wedding of his daughter (13).

Brokeback Mountain scores thirteen out of thirteen.

Erin Brockovich

Erin, an ex-beauty queen and single mother of three, needs a job, which is elusive because she has little education and people don't like the way she dresses (1). Erin was unable to follow her passion for medicine, biology and making the world a better place because she married an unreliable man while she was young and had kids (2). Erin is hit by a guy who runs a red light. With the help of a lawyer, Ed, she sues for medical expenses but loses (1). In desperation Erin goes to Ed's office and just starts working (3). Ed hires her and has her organize a pro bono real estate file that includes medical information (3). He also suggests Erin dress more appropriately. Erin retorts that she thinks she looks nice and thinks Ed's tie is tasteless (4). The neighbor, George, starts taking care of her kids as Erin works long hours driving out to the town near the PG&E factory, interviewing families, gaining their trust, researching at the Water Board, talking to toxicologists (5). Erin's kids are upset she is away so much and the secretaries treat Erin with disdain, but, out in the community, people start to respect her (5). When Erin is away for a week, Ed fires her, thinking she is out partying (6), then hires her back with a raise because Erin has learned PG&E has been dumping toxic Chromium 6 since the 1980s and over six hundred people are affected (5). This is potentially a multi-million-dollar settlement. However, multi-billion-dollar PG&E could drag out the proceedings, draining everything Ed has (9). When Ed and Erin win the right to go to trial, a big law firm comes on board and Erin is sidelined (6, 7). George begins to feel he is being used and tells Erin to choose between him and the job (9). Erin refuses to give up her work, which is bringing her respect (8). Ed has meetings without Erin in compliance with the new lawyers, George leaves Erin, so the kids have no babysitter, and the claimants start calling Erin because they distrust the new lawyers (9). The new lawyers take over the case, cutting out Erin (10). The community loses faith in the lawyers and starts to pull out (10). Erin puts her pride aside and helps Ed get the claimants back (11). George comes back to take care of the kids in the final push and Erin's son, recognizing the importance of her work, offers to bring Erin back some breakfast (12). A lonely guy tells Erin the information they need to connect the major corporation to the small-town operation (12). Erin presents the signed claims and the crucial information to the new lawyers, who stand with egg on their faces (11). The community wins the biggest environmental claim ever against a corporation and Erin and Ed take on other environmental cases (13).

Erin Brockovich scores thirteen out of thirteen.

Ever After

Danielle lives in the home of her deceased father, loved by the family servants and a slave to her stepmother Baroness Rodmilla De Ghent (1, 2). When a family servant, Maurice, is sold in payment for the Baroness's debts (3), Danielle decides to act on her values learned from her father's book *Utopia*, dress as a courtier (4), and buy Maurice back (3). The Prince happens by and supports Danielle, who cannot resist the opportunity to passionately point out to the Prince his failure to see the other people who place him so highly (3). The Prince finds this irresistible and keeps seeking her out (5) forcing Danielle to continue pretending to be Nicole de Lencret. They party with gypsies but Danielle fears her stepmother will discover she is not at home (5). With each encounter with the Prince, Danielle comes closer to being discovered (5). Finally, Danielle's confidence has grown to the point where she can no longer compliantly serve the Baroness (6). At a tea with the Queen, the Baroness realizes Danielle has been seeing the Prince (7). She locks Danielle in the cellar and takes her favored daughters to the ball. Danielle is disheartened (10) but with the help of Leonardo da Vinci goes to the ball where the Prince will announce who he will marry (11). Danielle is exposed as a fraud by the Baroness and rejected by the Prince (7). With nothing else to lose, Danielle bravely faces the Baroness and gives up hoping she will know the love of a mother from her (8). The Prince agrees to marry for political gain, Danielle is sold into slavery to a lecherous old man, and the servants and estate are left to the rule of the Baroness (9). Danielle frees herself from the old man (11) and meets the Prince on his way to save her. He has realized he loves her, regardless of her social class (12). He deeply regrets failing Danielle, and re-orders the kingdom to incorporate the values of *Utopia* (13).

Ever After scores thirteen out of thirteen.

Legally Blond

Elle Woods is Daddy's little rich girl who has found the man of her dreams, Warner, and believes he will propose, completing the plan for her perfect life (1). Warner, however, explains they have had loads of fun but he needs to marry someone serious because he plans to be a senator some day (2). But Elle Woods is no pushover. She gets accepted to Harvard Law School so Warner will see that she can be serious (anti-3). In front of her mirror, on her first day at law school, Elle puts on a pair of horn-rimmed glasses (4). Elle gets kicked out of class with the support of a horrible preppy girl who turns out to be Warner's fiancée, Vivian. Desperate for support, Elle speeds to a beauty salon. Her new friend convinces her to "steal the bastard back" (anti-3). Elle phones her friends in California for support but they care only about getting married and their hair (6). Undaunted, Elle goes to a party, only to find Warner will never consider her smart (8). Elle gives up trying to get married and applies herself to law school (8). One day, Elle puts on her glasses (3) to impersonate a lawyer and help her friend get back her dog (5). She really likes the feeling of being taken seriously and helping people. Elle gets an internship to help defend a fitness guru, Brooke, accused of murdering her husband (5). Just when she believes the world sees she has serious potential, her law professor/boss makes a pass at her (7). Suddenly, she sees what a joke she has been to everyone and feels they will never see beyond her looks (anti-8). Elle quits the firm and packs to go back to California (anti-11) but her female law professor, who once kicked her out of class, says "If you are going to let one prick ruin your life, then you are not the girl I thought you were" (12). Meanwhile, Brooke is in real trouble (9). Emmett, a lawyer who is rooting for Elle to channel her power as a blond towards the greater good, comes up with a plan (12). Brooke fires her lawyer and hires Elle with the support of Emmett (12). Elle dresses as herself, pretty in pink (4), and steps up to the challenge (11). At first Elle asks stupid questions and the team starts to lose faith in her (10), but then Elle's knowledge of perms reveals the witness is lying and she proves Brooke's innocence (13). Two years later, Elle is class valedictorian. She is a shining example of the importance of looking beyond first impressions, having passion in the law, and always having faith in yourself (13).

Legally Blond scores thirteen out of thirteen. The Back and Forth element of the **Secret World** is only weakly developed when she puts on her glasses to get her friend's dog back.

Maid in Manhattan

Marisa is a chambermaid who lives with her mother and son in the projects of Manhattan (1). As a maid, Marisa must take care of the whims of the rich and be invisible (2). One day Marisa is pushed by a friend to try on a five-thousand-dollar Dolce suit (4) and is mistaken by a senatorial candidate, Chris, as a fellow guest (3). They go for a walk and Marisa's picture ends up on the front page of the newspaper (6). Marisa fears she will be fired rather than promoted to management (5). Chris is charmed by Marisa's socialist views and straightforwardness, and pulls strings to get a date with her (5). Meanwhile, a management position opens up in the hotel and Marisa's friend sends in Marisa's application (3). Marisa gains confidence from being with Chris and believes she can prove her mother wrong and reach for a management position (8). She borrows a gown (4) and goes to the charity ball to tell Chris she cannot see him anymore in order to secure her new job. Marisa stays the night with Chris, forgetting she is a maid in that hotel (6), is discovered by a guest in the morning, and revealed as a guest impersonator (7). The press has a field day on her fight with Chris (10). Marisa is fired, Chris fades away to focus on his campaign, and Marisa's mother asserts that people like them must remember their place (10). Marisa's supervisor quits working at the hotel in solidarity with Marisa, and the maids lose their hope that one of them will make management (9). Marisa stands up for herself, asserting she will start over at a new hotel and in a few years she will try again to make management (11). Chris comes back into town and Marisa's son asks Chris to give Marisa another chance (12). Marisa becomes a manager and promotes other chambermaids to management positions as she dates Chris (13).

Maid In Manhattan scores thirteen out of thirteen, but the **Re-ordering** is done by the son, making the love interest look weak.

Miss Congeniality

Gracie Hart is a tough, smart, undercover cop who fits in with her co-workers by being one of the guys (1). She secretly likes her co-worker Eric Mathews but has no feminine wiles to get his romantic attention (2). When a serial killer, The Citizen, sends a message that he is targeting the Miss America pageant, Gracie is assigned to be an undercover beauty pageant contestant (3). Gracie is transformed into a beauty through the work of Mr. Victor, a long-time veteran of the pageant industry (4). Gracie almost blows her cover eating pizza at will and sneaking out to meet Eric and Mr. Victor (5). Gracie comes to see the beauty contestants are smart, kind, and ambitious people (8). When Mr. Victor tells Gracie she is an incomplete person with sarcasm and a gun instead of friends and relationships, Gracie quits. She doesn't know who she is any more (6). She agrees to continue for Eric's sake but when the FBI catches The Citizen, the team pulls out of the Miss America Pageant (10). Gracie feels this is a copycat crime and her girls are still in danger. Gracie hands in her badge and continues with the pageant (10). Mr. Victor can't stay but he tells Gracie he has never been more proud of a client and he leaves her a gown (12). Eric learns from Mr. Victor that the contest organizer is being fired and her son, who works with her, has a criminal record. Eric rejoins Gracie and together they try to protect the contestants (12). Gracie makes a gracious speech about her fellow contestants declaring she will protect her girls as she continues in the contest (11) and suddenly realizes the bomb is in the crown. Gracie grabs the crown as it is being placed on the winner's head, the new queen fights back thinking this is a case of really bad sportsmanship (7), while Eric wrestles the son for the remote detonator. Gracie throws the crown into the air as it explodes (9). The pageant contestants are saved (13). Gracie is recognized by Eric as a good cop and a loveable woman, and Gracie embraces her femininity as the most liberating experience of her life as she receives the Miss Congeniality Award (8, 12).

Miss Congeniality scores thirteen out of thirteen.

New Waterford Girl

Moonie lives in an isolated Maritime town with her mother, father, and five brothers and sisters. They are simple, God-fearing people who work in the mines, marry, have children, and never leave town (1). Moonie longs to go to art school in New York but her family sees her becoming a nurse, giving her drugs to help calm her rebellious nature (2). One day Moonie sees a pregnant unwed girl, Tammy, sent out of town to have the kid (3). Moonie decides to act like a tramp, fake pregnancy, and get sent away so she can use her New York art school scholarship (5). Moonie wears pants instead of her little-girl dresses (4) and flirts with several guys. Everyone wants to know what's going on (6). She confesses she is pregnant, breaking away from her habit of pleasing her family (8) and losing her bond with her mother (6). Moonie is almost caught when the boys talk to each other and discover none of them did the deed (5). Her friend, Lou, who can make a guilty guy fall with a single punch, agrees to box in exchange for the boys' silence (12). In the end, a boy tells Moonie's dad the truth to save her (7, false 12). Moonie's dad then figures the culprit has to be Moonie's teacher, who clearly has a crush on her, and goes after him (anti-12). The teacher pretends he is the culprit to secure Moonie's freedom (half-12). Moonie kisses her teacher in front of everyone to seal her future (11) and finds herself ostracized by her family, sad to be leaving her best friend Lou, and suddenly appreciative of all she has in her hometown (10). Moonie's brother calls her a slut and is confused by why she is leaving (9), her teacher's trailer is pushed off a cliff by Moonie's mother (half 12), and Tammy stays in town to have her baby (9). Dad decides to bake a cake and invites Moonie to sit with the family and neighbors and have a big slice (half 12). Desolately, Moonie gets on the train at her mother's insistence (12). On the train, Moonie reads a letter from her mother explaining she knows Moonie is not pregnant and will straighten it out with everyone before she comes back (12).

New Waterford Girl scores twelve out of thirteen. There is no scene showing the benefit to the community for Moonie's having followed her dream.

Pretty Woman

Vivian is a sex-trade worker who protects herself with a code that includes no kissing on the mouth, and she says who, she says when, and she says how (1). But the street is dangerous and, without a pimp's protection, Vivian is vulnerable to the fate of a fellow worker found dead in a dumpster (1). One day a rich man, Edward, looking for directions, picks Vivian up in his Lotus and offers to hire her for a week to attend business events with him (3). Vivian accepts the work for five thousand dollars and goes shopping but nobody will serve her (2) until Edward takes her shopping on Rodeo Drive (4). At her first dinner party Vivian is charming and shows her special talents for being down to earth, relating to people, and building business relationships (5). At a polo match Edward tells his business partner, Philip, Vivian is a hooker (5). Vivian feels hurt (6). As Vivian grows closer to Edward, she stops believing that she is only deserving of "bums," and refuses to allow Edward to hurt her (8). The week comes to an end and Edward offers to keep Vivian in an apartment (anti-12). Vivian refuses (11) and must face living on the Boulevard again (10). Vivian inspires Edward to change the way he does business, and a new type of relationship with a more humane business deal is created (13). Philip is outraged (7) and attacks Vivian looking for retribution (10). Edward arrives, beats Phillip off Vivian and sees him for the creep that he is (false 12). Vivian goes back to her apartment on the Boulevard to pack to go to school (10). Edward finds Vivian, overcomes his fear of heights (and commitment), and offers Vivian marriage (12).

Pretty Woman scores thirteen out of thirteen. **The Kingdom Is Brighter** is largely Edward's doing, only inspired by Vivian. This would have been a stronger Virgin story if Vivian had gone to business school and continued to develop her skills with people in business.

Shakespeare in Love

Viola De Lesseps is a beautiful-rich-girl-without-pedigree betrothed to Lord Wessex, a man she does not love, to increase her family's social position (1, 2). Viola longs to know passion through the theater but British law declares it illegal for women to perform on the stage (2). However, the plague has caused the theaters to close and the actors to travel. When the playhouse suddenly opens, amateurs are offered a chance to act (3). Viola's parents have gone away for three weeks, so Viola dresses as a boy (4) and wins a male role in Shakespeare's new play, *Romeo and Juliet*. Shakespeare meets Viola as a woman and falls instantly in love with her (5). They become lovers and play a dangerous game with Viola as a boy in Will's play in the day and the woman he makes love to at night (5). One day Viola must meet the Queen for approval to marry Lord Wessex (2). The Queen sees Viola no longer has the blush of a virgin and tells Wessex (7). Meanwhile, Viola is furious to discover Will is married and refuses to see him anymore (6). At rehearsal, a vengeful boy puts a mouse in

Viola's shirt to reveal her as a woman (7). Viola is banished from the play (10). When Marlowe, a fellow writer, dies, Shakespeare believes he is to blame, and Viola is mistakenly told Will is dead (9). Viola recognizes the folly of her anger and admits she loves Will beyond poetry (8). Reunited with Will, Viola gives up her notions of romantic happiness, and takes whatever form of love she and Will can have (8) before she must marry Lord Wessex and move to the Americas (10). When the female lead in the play loses his voice, Viola stands in and plays Juliet despite the law (11). She is charged with the crime (10) but the Queen stands up for her (12) and Viola realizes her dream of being a stage actress. The world has a new play and women are soon permitted to perform on the stage (13).

Shakespeare in Love scores thirteen out of thirteen.

Sister Act

Deloris is a lounge singer in a Vegas casino owned by her married gangster-boyfriend (1). She's not happy because she wants to be a legitimate wife and singer (2). When her boyfriend gifts Deloris his wife's fur coat, Deloris goes to tell him it is over and accidentally walks in on a murder which puts Deloris on her boyfriend's hit list (3). In the witness protection program Deloris is placed in a convent, dressed as a nun (4), which is the last place anyone would look for her (5). In the convent, Deloris is put in charge of the choir and draws the neighborhood in with her music (5). The church is revitalized as people are inspired by Deloris's music to attend the church and clean up their community (5). Deloris decides to stop trying to be famous and think about what her music means to other people (8). Deloris draws the media (6) and the cops want to relocate her but Deloris won't abandon the nuns right before the Pope is coming to hear them sing (9). Deloris's boyfriend finds out where she is and snatches her (7). The nuns decide they don't care that they were lied to and had a lounge singer among them and they fly to the casino (9) to rescue Deloris (12). The gangsters won't kill Deloris because she looks like a nun. Deloris keeps talking like a nun (10) until the nuns and cops arrive and save her (12). Deloris leads the choir as they sing for the Pope (11). The convent is saved and Doris and the nuns put out several successful albums (13).

Sister Act scores thirteen out of thirteen.

The Sound of Music

Maria is an apprentice nun who has lived in a convent since she left her family in the mountains (1). The nuns love her but cannot get her to stop singing and running through the hills (2). The Mother Superior decides to send her to help Captain von Trapp of the Austrian army to help take care of his seven children (3). They clash instantly as Maria refuses to whistle for the children in military fashion and instead makes play clothes from her curtains (4). Together, Maria and the children sing and explore the mountains and grow to love each other (5), until the Captain comes back with his new fiancée, the Baroness (7). Maria blushes when she dances with the Captain, and runs back to the convent when the Baroness recognizes Maria is in love with the Captain (6). Nothing is right anymore, the children sing without joy and the Nazis are moving into the country (9). Maria talks to the Mother Superior and is told the church is not a place to hide (10). Maria goes back to the von Trapps and faces the Captain, who declares he is in love with her, too (11). They marry and after their honeymoon come home to find the Captain must report to the Nazis, which he cannot morally do (9). The von Trapp family decides to escape to Switzerland (11). They are caught sneaking away and use singing in the community competition, reminding Austrians of their proud heritage (13), as a cover for their escape. The nuns help them (12) and the family crosses the mountains to Switzerland on foot, where they live to sing and tell their story (13).

The Sound of Music scores thirteen out of thirteen.

Strictly Ballroom

Scott Hastings is a star dancer being groomed to succeed in the world of ballroom dancing. There was no doubt in his mother's mind that Scott and Liz would be the next Amateur Grand Champions (1). But Scott wants to experiment with his own steps (2). His coach tells Scott to stop getting above himself; the people who invented those steps knew a lot more than he did; Scott will never win if he doesn't conform (2). During competition, Scott gets "boxed in" and uses his own steps to break free. Liz quits as his partner, opening up try-outs for a new partner (3). Fran, a beginner, approaches Scott, offering to dance non-Federation steps with him in the Pan Pacifics (3). Fran and Scott secretly practice at night, developing their own steps (5), while by day Scott goes along with the try-outs arranged by his mother and coach (5). Scott is beginning to fall in love with Fran (6). When Tina Sparkle becomes available as Scott's partner his mother is delighted, and Scott sees the chance to actually win. Scott tries to discuss it with Fran. They start to dance and everyone sees Scott has been grooming a beginner to dance new steps with him (7). Fran is sent home and Tina meets Scott (anti-11) but eventually Scott decides he's going to dance his own steps with Fran instead (11). He runs to Fran to tell her, and faces Fran's family. Fran's father challenges Scott to dance. Arrogantly Scott accepts, only to be laughed at (7). Fran's grandmother and father teach Scott how to give up his cocky style and dance from his heart (8). The Federation president pulls Scott aside and tells him the secret of his father's failure and his mother's disappointment. He says Scott's father was a great dancer but he did his own steps and lost. Now he wants Scott to win for the both of them. Scott doesn't know who his allegiance is strongest towards, Fran or his dad (10). He agrees to dance with Liz and win for his dad, only to find it doesn't matter how he dances because the completion is fixed for another team (9). Dad breaks through the defenses of the club members and tells Scott the Federation president lied.

He never took the chance to dance his step and always regretted it – it is the dancing that matters (8, 12). Scott dons Fran's father's matador vest (4) and steps on the floor with Fran (11). The Federation tries to stop them but Scott's dad claps Scott and Fran forward and the crowd gets behind them (12). The new steps are a hit (13)! Love is in the air as Scott's mother and dad heal their long-standing rift, and the dancing community feels a new passion for dance (13).

Strictly Ballroom scores thirteen out of thirteen.

The Virgin Suicides

Lux lives in a world where her sister has committed suicide because of the strictness of their parents (2). They comply with house rules and become objects of curiosity in their town (1). One day Trig falls for Lux and arranges to take Lux and her sisters to the homecoming dance (3). They all make new dresses that their mom makes look like sacks (failed 4). Trig offers Lux a secret world of passion (5). She takes the opportunity (6), only to be left alone on the football field the morning after and shamed by her family when she cabs home (7). Her mother makes Lux burn her rock and roll records (2) and pulls all the sisters out of school so they live in complete isolation with no hope (10). Her father goes insane and a news station reports that suicide among girls is a trend (9). Abandoned by Trig (failed 12), Lux goes into her shadow side and plays the whore on the roof (failed 8). The sisters all commit suicide (failed 11) and the boys who find them are never able to understand it or get on with their lives (failed 13).

The Virgin Suicides scores thirteen out of thirteen with several beats failing which makes the story a tragedy.

Wedding Crashers

John, an orphan, pretends to be a wedding guest with his friend Jeremy to experience family love and get girls to sleep with them while avoiding the horrors of marriage they see in their jobs as divorce mediators (1). But John is starting to question whether he is a sleazy, irresponsible, dirty old man (2). When the biggest wedding of the year comes up, John decides he will crash one more wedding with Jeremy. What John didn't expect was to meet Claire, a disarmingly authentic woman (3). John wrangles an invitation to the family retreat, where he wears the family's clothes (4) for a series of traditional activities. Despite a jealous boyfriend and a protective father watch-dogging him, and several near discoveries, John reveals his true self to Claire and they start to connect (5). John tells Jeremy he thinks he is falling in love, which is against the crasher rules (6). Meanwhile, Claire's boyfriend hires an investigator who reveals John and Jeremy are wedding crashers (7). John and Jeremy are kicked out of the family retreat at gunpoint and Claire won't respond to John's phone calls. Jeremy is suddenly always busy and John ends up crashing weddings on his own (10). No longer a pleasant addition to the celebrations, John preaches that love and friendship don't exist (anti-8). John goes into a depression made worse by the announcement of Jeremy's wedding to Claire's sister (10). John progresses to attending funerals, where he comes face-to-face with how pathetic his life has become (10). As he watches the widow, John realizes everyone will eventually lose the ones they love, but he doesn't have to lose Claire right now (8). He wants to know love while he can. John goes to Claire, at Jeremy's wedding, and tells her he loves her and wants to date her (11). Claire's fiancé attacks John, and Jeremy clocks him, proving friendship does exist (12). Claire's father affirms he will accept whomever his daughter loves (12). In the end, John and Claire's souls have found their counterpoint in another. By being authentic, they have found true love (13).

Wedding Crashers scores thirteen out of thirteen.

While You Were Sleeping

Lucy grew up with her dad, keeping her mother's memory alive with stories. Now that her dad has died, Lucy lives alone, keeping her father's memory alive by wearing his old clothes and telling their stories (1). Being the only one without family, Lucy works all the holidays (2). Each day at her job in the subway, Lucy watches a beautiful man, Peter, go through her turnstile and imagines they are in love. One day, Peter is mugged and left unconscious on the train tracks as a train approaches (3). Lucy jumps on the tracks and saves Peter's life. At the hospital, Lucy allows herself to be assumed to be Peter's fiancée as he lies in a coma (5). Peter's family is delighted he has finally found a nice girl (5). Peter's brother, Jack, is suspicious and sets out to prove Lucy is not Peter's girlfriend (5). Lucy has a gift for relationships and inspires Jack to talk to his dad and tell him he wants to leave the family business (5). Lucy loves being in the family but Jack is close to finding out she does not belong (5), and she is starting to fall in love with Jack (6). To further complicate things, the family friend, Saul, discovers Lucy's secret and tells her Jack's Gram has a bad heart and the shock of loosing Lucy might kill her (5). Finally, Peter comes out of his coma (7). When he doesn't recognize Lucy, his family declares Peter to have amnesia and on the advice of his family, Peter asks Lucy to marry him. Lucy accepts because she wants this family and isn't willing to live with just her memories anymore (8). She dresses the part of the bride (4) because she is ready to take action over dreams. Unfortunately, Lucy does not love Peter, but Jack refuses to admit he loves Lucy (10). At the altar, Lucy confesses her deceit and her true feelings for Jack (11). She chooses to wait for true love and goes back to face her lonely life (10). Just then a horrible woman shows up claiming to be Peter's real fiancée, followed by her husband, and for a moment it looks like Gram is going to have that heart attack (9). Alone again, Lucy gives notice at her job and makes plans to go to

Europe (10). Jack shows up at the subway ticket window, with his family behind him, and pays the price to ask Lucy to marry him (12). Jack and Lucy honeymoon in Europe and the family is bound together by another generation of true love (13).

While You Were Sleeping scores thirteen out of thirteen.

Working Girl

Tess is a secretary in a dead-end job where her male co-workers pimp her to keep her from competing with them (1). When she fights back a little she is told by HR to get along or she'll lose her job (2). Tess is assigned to a new boss, Catherine, who says she is open to Tess's ideas and advises her to "make it happen" (3). When Catherine is laid up in Europe with a broken leg, Tess discovers Catherine has been stealing Tess's idea. Tess decides to leave her dead-beat boyfriend, and move into Catherine's life to promote her idea (3). Tess wears Catherine's classy designer dress and heads out to a business party to network (4). She meets Jack, and teams up with him to sell Mr. Trask on Tess's idea, narrowly avoiding being recognized by Catherine's friends (5). Tess's friends pressure her to make up with her old boy-friend but she won't allow herself to be ordered up like steak anymore (6). Catherine comes back to the office and gives Tess a reasonable explanation as to why she appeared to be promoting Tess's idea as her own. This time Tess gives up her nice-girl passivity and decides to cross-check Catherine's story (8). She learns it was a lie. Tess goes to the meeting to close the deal. Catherine barges in and accuses Tess of stealing her idea and exposes Tess as a secretary (7). Tess loses her job and Jack (10). Tess runs into Jack, Catherine, and Mr. Trask at the elevator and decides to stand up for herself and prove it was her idea (11). There is mass confusion and it looks like the deal will fall apart, along with Jack's career (9). Jack decides to stand by Tess, telling Mr. Trask to "hear the lady out" (12). Mr. Trask recognizes that Tess is a bright worker, believes her over Catherine, and gives her a job in his company (12). Tess forms a new relationship with her secretary, and the girls in the secretary pool have hope for advancement in the future (13).

Working Girl scores thirteen out of thirteen.

Chapter 3

Anti-Virgin Stories

*A*n anti-Virgin story reverses the roles of the Virgin and the kingdom: the Virgin is driven to suppress her inner nature or dream and her community is pushing her to bring her true self to life. *Mamma Mia!* and *The 40 Year Old Virgin* are both anti-Virgin stories. Sophie needs to follow her passion for life against her own wishes. Andy needs to overcome his fear of humiliation and let go of his protective behaviors. In both cases, the people around them encourage the archetypal transformation while the protagonist is holding herself back.

In *Mamma Mia!* Sophie is in love with Sky, but rather than exploring the world together and getting to know herself, she wants to get married and help build her mom's business. Coincidentally, this was the dream of her mother, Donna. Donna had fallen in love with Sam twenty years earlier and taken him to her special island. Sam, a budding architect, had envisioned a hotel on the island where they could spend their lives together. Sam ended up going back to America and marrying someone else while Donna built the hotel and raised their secret love child as a single mom. Sophie is a Virgin who is so grateful and loving towards Donna that she won't leave her. Getting married and helping Donna run the hotel has become Sophie's **Dependent World**.

In *The 40 Year Old Virgin*, Andy was traumatized by his early attempts to become sexually active. His **Dependent World** is the complex Andy has developed to protect him from further humiliation. Andy collects and plays with action figures, comic books, and video games; exercises to sublimate his natural urges; and avoids close male friendships to keep his secret from getting out.

The **Price of Conformity** is disharmony with the kingdom. The anti-Virgin wants to conform and the kingdom is pushing her to grow. In *Mamma Mia!* Donna thinks Sky is great but secretly hopes Sophie will call off the wedding and experience freedom from the responsibilities of life. She is worried that Sophie is worrying too much about her and not enough about Sophie. In *The 40 Year Old Virgin*, Andy's complex is working very well to protect him from the awkwardness of a first sexual encounter and the social stigma of being a virgin. People just think he's some kind of social deviant. But Andy's complex is not allowing him to have a fulfilling life. He is alone, stuck in juvenile behavior and very frustrated.

The **Opportunity to Shine** for Sophie is when she finds Donna's diary and discovers the names of her three possible fathers. She determines to meet her dad and know who she is. She crafts a plan to invite them all to her wedding. This is an anti-Virgin **Opportunity to Shine** because it is based on the principle that someone else can tell her who she is.

When Andy is invited to play poker with David, Cal and Jay, it is his **Opportunity to Shine** and he takes it. They are having fun with lots of male banter until it becomes obvious that Andy has never had sex. His new friends determine that they have to help him get over the first hurdle and Andy is somewhat resistant.

Dresses the Part in the anti-Virgin story is dressing the wrong part. In *Mamma Mia!* Sophie spends a moment in front of the mirror with her friends holding up her wedding dress but never puts it on. There is a disconnection between her and the symbol of marriage. Andy sits alone in his apartment, in *The 40 Year Old Virgin*, playing his video games and admiring his action figures (which are never taken out of the box) when Dave drops by with porn. He tells Andy all his toys have to go because they will turn women off. Borrowing porn and doing what others tell him to do in order to have sex is the opposite of the intention of **Dresses the Part**. Rather than illuminating his true self he is covering it up by taking other people's advice on how to get a girl.

In the **Secret World**, Sophie moves back and forth between getting to know her potential dads, one of whom is Sam, and preparing for her wedding with Sky, always fearful Donna will discover she has invited her potential dads to her wedding. When Donna discovers her old boyfriends, Sophie makes the father candidates say they know nothing of the wedding, to keep Sophie's plan a secret. The secret, however, is working against the Virgin, allowing her to maintain a misguided sense of what she needs from life, namely that knowing who her dad is will tell her who she is.

In *The 40 Year Old Virgin*, Andy moves back and forth between trying the suggestions Dave, Cal and Jay have for him to get laid and retreating to his apartment (the **Secret World** where he will never grow). Andy meets Trish and finds he really cares for her (another **Opportunity to Shine**). Through clever second-date banter they agree to have twenty dates before they have sex. This time becomes the **Secret World**. Andy grows in his comfort with Trish, while trying to keep his virginity a secret.

No Longer Fits Her World in *Mamma Mia!* finds Sophie distressed to learn that she can't tell which man is her dad. Meeting them didn't tell her anything. She thought she would recognize him instantly and know who she is. Now things are not fitting together.

Andy has finished his twenty dates with Trish and she is ready to have sex with him, in *The 40 Year Old Virgin*. Andy freaks because his life is changing too fast with this and Trish selling all his action figures so Andy can start his own business.

Caught Shining is the moment when the **Secret World** and the **Dependent World** collide. In the Anti-Virgin story, it is the moment when the Virgin's faulty thinking is exposed. Sophie tells Sky her three potential dads are here and he is angry that the wedding is more about finding her dad than their love. He tells her that he agreed to the whole white wedding because he wanted what she wanted but now he is not so sure.

Anti-Caught Shining in *Mamma Mia!*

In *The 40 Year Old Virgin*, **Caught Shining** occurs after Andy **Wanders in the Wilderness** at a bar. His world then goes into chaos when Trish discovers porn and a plastic vagina in Andy's apartment and thinks Andy is planning to kill her. She jumps in her car and drives away.

Now the Virgin story and anti-Virgin story have joined the same path. Andy is again **Wandering in the Wilderness** as he chases Trish on his bike, takes a short cut and ends up catapulting over her car and through a truck billboard. Trish runs to his side and Andy tells her he is a virgin (**Gives Up What Kept Him Stuck**). Andy fears Trish will think he is weird but she is just glad he isn't planning to kill her. Andy realizes being a virgin doesn't make him weird. He was just waiting for the right person (**Chooses His Light**). Andy and Trish get married, surrounded by Jay, Dave, and Cal, who now have love partners, and Andy makes half a million dollars selling his action figures (**The Kingdom Is Brighter**).

In *Mamma Mia!* Sophie asks Donna to give her away because she recognizes she must leave Donna to find herself. They have been so close through her growing up she has previously been unable to let go (**Gives Up What Kept Her Stuck**).

Sky is no longer sure about going along with what Sophie wants, and Sophie has three men expecting to give her away and is no closer to knowing who she is (**Wanders in the Wilderness**). In the church, Donna's sordid past is revealed and three men stand up as Sophie's father, and declare they are happy to have one third of Sophie (**Kingdom in Chaos**). Sophie suddenly knows what she wants. She asks Sky to forget the wedding and go see the world with her (**Chooses Her Light**). Sam asks Donna to marry him, which frees Sophie to live her own life (**Re-ordering**). Sophie leaves to explore Europe and Donna begins her life with Sam. The **Kingdom Is Brighter** as Sam and Donna build on their original dream, owning a hotel together on their special island. Sophie began on the wrong path but ended up making the world right for everyone.

The anti-Virgin technique can be used as a single beat in a movie as well. *Legally Blond* follows a Virgin structure until Elle's boss makes a pass at her and she quits her job and Harvard law school. She adopts the view that she really is a joke. Rather than **Giving Up What Kept Her Stuck**, she adopts what kept her stuck. This anti-beat makes it more poignant when Elle later enters the courtroom dressed in pink and assumes the role of lead council.

Chapter 4

The Hero Archetypal Journey

*I*n the process of writing *The Virgin's Promise*, the Hero gained definition relative to the Virgin. He has gone from representing all stories, to being one half of the process to know independence. This section provides a summary of the Hero's journey as described in Christopher Vogler's *The Writer's Journey* and Joseph Campbell's *The Hero with a Thousand Faces* modestly refined by distinctions and emphases made clear by understanding the Virgin as his counterpart. The role of feminine archetypes such as the Crone and the Virgin in his journey are also noted in this summary. .

The essence of the Hero's story is that he must prove to himself that he can leave the comforts and security of home, face death, and expand the boundaries of his mortality. He does this by selflessly venturing to a foreign land to save his village.

The twelve beats of the Hero's Journey can be summarized as:

1. Ordinary World
2. Call to Adventure
3. Refusal of the Call
4. Meeting with the Guide
5. Crossing the First Threshold

6. Tests, Allies, Enemies
7. Preparations
8. Crisis
9. Reward
10. The Road Back
11. Final Battle
12. Return with the Elixir

Stage One: Ordinary World

There are three main things the **Ordinary World** stage must accomplish: the Hero's comfort zone, the basic goodness of the village, and the Hero's character including the complex that holds him back.

THE HERO'S COMFORT ZONE

The Hero's **Ordinary World** sets the baseline for his familiar and/or comfortable life, sometimes to the point of boredom or frustration. The Hero is in a position of safety and nurturance, entwined in his Mother Complex. He is fed, clothed, and soothed in this environment. Even if money is tight or a loved one has died, the Hero is comfortable because the situation is known to him and his survival is not threatened.

In *The Matrix*, Thomas Anderson is a program writer with a respectable software company in 1999. He lives in a small apartment dominated by computer equipment and helps his neighbor with the garbage each week. He also lives in an underground software world under the name Neo and has a nagging feeling he is waiting to wake up from a dream.

The **Ordinary World** is defined by its high contrast to the foreign land that the Hero eventually goes to. The greater the contrast, the greater the Hero's discomfort, and the more compelling the story. The Hero goes from a sedentary life in a peaceful village, to the constant relocation and chaos of a war zone (*Lord of the Rings, Willow*); from a safe apartment in New York City to a jungle in South America (*Romancing the Stone*); from a Detroit police force where the cops bust their own sting operation to a Los Angeles police force where the chain of authority is highly respected (*Beverly Hills Cop*); from the theoretical world of a law student to an affluent and high-stakes life with the law firm (*The Firm*). The **Ordinary World** shows us the Hero at home living normally before the adventure begins.

THE HERO'S CONNECTION TO HIS VILLAGE

In a Hero story the **Ordinary World** is basically good, and deserves to be protected and sustained. It is orderly, peaceful, or nurturing. The Hero has people who love him or someone he loves, such as a dead parent, or is surrounded by values that are worth preserving. It is the metaphoric womb, the mother, and is worth fighting for.

Blood Diamond opens with a good African man, Solomon, and his loving wife and children in rural Sierra Leone. Their world is peaceful with strong values of family including Solomon supporting his son, Dia, in becoming a doctor and contributing to his community.

In *Unforgiven*, William Munny is a widower struggling in a bleak land to raise two kids with the good values his beloved, departed wife impressed upon him. He works hard to separate himself from his gunslinger days in gratitude to his wife for having loved him despite his wicked nature.

Love for a woman is also the driving force in *The Princess Bride*. Westley is a farmhand in a lovely pastoral setting and feels the greatest love of all time for the farmer's daughter, Buttercup. Willow has the love of his wife and children, in a village where he farms the land that provides for his family (*Willow*).

The mark of an **Ordinary World** is that, in its core, it is not in need of change. The **Ordinary World** establishes the Hero's attachment to the village and the pull to save it when it is threatened. However, from the beginning to the end of the movie, the only substantive change to the village will be the end of the threat to its peaceful continuation.

THE HERO'S COMPLEX

Time spent in the **Ordinary World** is a chance to get to know the Hero, including his character and his weakness. The protagonist's complex gives depth to the Hero's journey, increasing the conflict as it encourages avoidance and inaction while the archetype drives towards risking death to know he can stand alone.

Generally, key events in the Hero's life have shaped his character. For example, in *Back to the Future*, Marty is the son of George McFly, who always backs down from confrontation. This has made Marty over-reactive. He keeps getting sidetracked from his purpose because he jumps in too soon to take action.

As the agents come to get Neo in *The Matrix*, and Morpheus is directing his escape, Neo mumbles his complex. "Why is this happening? Why me? I'm nobody. I didn't do anything." He needs to let go of these beliefs before he can be successful in his journey.

Blood Diamond opens with rural life in Sierra Leone. Danny is a smuggler living by his wits in the beautiful countryside of Africa. He fits in with the landscape and is clever in his ability to work the system. After losing his parents in the bloody battles for control of the country's rich natural resources, Danny was taken in by a manipulative colonel who used him for his own gain. As a result, Danny is very street smart and lives by a code of non-attachment, looking after no one but himself.

In these scenarios we learn about the Hero's complex, which will be challenged in order for the Hero to complete his journey. The complex generally encourages the Hero to stay comfortable, think about himself, doubt his potential or avoid pain because these are the qualities that must be eliminated for him to fulfill the masculine journey of going to a foreign land to be rugged, selfless, skilled, and brave as he expands the physical space in which he knows he can thrive.

Stage Two: Call to Adventure

In the **Call to Adventure**, the peace and order of the **Ordinary World** are threatened and the Hero is called upon to secure it. The village must be protected, provided for, or sometimes restored. This **Call to Adventure** can take the form of notification of an impending attack, a wrong which must be set right, temptation or restlessness, or something needed from the outside.

NOTIFICATION OF AN IMPENDING ATTACK

Often the villain, or his henchman, makes a reconnaissance tour of the village to plan his invasion or get information. Someone in the village spots the evil force and gives the village an early warning.

In *Star Wars*, Darth Vader is working to get the rebel spies under control before using the Death Star to annihilate a planet. Princess Leia is able to steal the blueprints for the Death Star, which may give the rebel fighters a chance to discern its weakness. The plans end up in the hands of Luke Skywalker, giving Luke an early warning that his galaxy is under threat.

In a more subtle context, Abby tells Mitch she finds it creepy that the wives are subtly controlled by the firm's policy that states "wives are not forbidden to work and children are encouraged" (*The Firm*). Mitch has his eyes on money and social status, and fails to heed the warning.

In *Willow*, a baby is found floating down the river in a basket. Advance notice is being given of an epic adventure where a great future leader must be saved to ensure the longevity of the village, reminiscent of Moses. When the evil queen's soldiers and wild boars terrorize the village, looking for a baby, there is another early warning of the threat to the future of the village and the larger region.

A Wrong Must Be Set Right

The **Call to Adventure** may be a wrong which must be set right. The peace and order of the village can be enjoyed only if justice reigns. When an evil deed has gone unpunished, it must be corrected before the village will be at ease again. The wrong may be an act of brutality against the helpless, a rape, a murder, a theft, or the breaking of a code.

In *Unforgiven*, a whore was brutally disfigured because she giggled at the size of a client's member. When the local sheriff compensates the whorehouse owner for loss of income and calls it square, the whores are outraged. They secretly put up a bounty for the death of the two men who committed this crime against them. When the Schofield Kid comes to William Munny looking for a killing partner, William says, "I guess they've got it coming to them." It is a wrong that must be righted.

In *Thelma and Louise*, when a man attempts to rape Thelma, Louise is called upon to take action. The wrongs done to her in the past were not sufficiently addressed and come flooding back to her as she holds a gun on the rapist. Louise pulls the trigger, setting up the moral dilemma of a hierarchy of wrong. Which is more worthy of righting: the wrong against this man, the past wrong against Louise, or the wrongs against women in society?

Temptation and Restlessness

The Hero is sometimes restless in his skin, surrounded by safe predictability, with no adventure in which he can prove his bravery; he yearns to know the boundaries of his mortality. There may be the temptation of buried treasure, great honor, or great wealth that causes the Hero to expand his world.

Three sons of a military hero, raised in a prosperous Midwestern United States family, learn of the war in Europe (*Legends of the Fall*). The youngest son decides to enlist, eager to distinguish himself on the battlefield like his father. Similar themes of the pull of the military are found in *An Officer and a Gentlemen* and *Top Gun*.

Another temptation of the Hero may be a prize for winning a race, a treasure or a love. In *Pirates of the Caribbean*, Jack embarks on a life-threatening adventure for the chance to find the greatest pirate stash and get back his ship, the *Black Pearl*. Will seeks to win the prize of Elizabeth's love by proving his worthiness.

SOMETHING IS NEEDED FROM THE OUTSIDE

A lack or a need of the village may call the Hero to adventure. Any loss, such as the loss of health, security or love, is this type of motivation. If the crops are failing because there has been no rain, the Hero is called upon to fetch back the rainmaker. If the village lacks females to sustain the population the Hero must go out and find a good woman to bring back home. Some factor from the outside is needed to ensure the continued existence of the village.

In *Blood Diamond*, Sierra Leone is torn apart by warmongers fighting for control of the diamond-rich territory. They are secretly financed by diamond buyers who are using sanctions to drive the price of diamonds up while they hoard smuggled diamonds. Sierra Leone's future requires someone to expose the activities of the diamond buyers and the warring factions. Danny, a diamond smuggler, is called upon to give information that will expose the diamond consortium and cut off the supply of money and weapons from the outside.

Stage Three: Refusal of the Call

The shadow side of the Hero, the Coward, makes an appearance in the **Refusal of the Call**. When first asked to leave his cozy village, the Hero is quick with reasons why he couldn't possibly go. His family needs him, the job is too big, it's certain suicide, someone else is better suited for the task, he has obligations, he's not that stupid!

The **Refusal of the Call** expresses what's at stake for the Hero. It is an opportunity to spell out the grave dangers that lie ahead and the many ways the Hero could die an excruciatingly painful death. The tension can be increased by several characters refusing the call, each with another good reason for not going.

William (*Unforgiven*) refuses to go until he sees it is a way to save his children from their current poverty. He then invites Ned to come along. Ned refuses on the moral grounds that killing is wrong and William's deceased wife would not approve. As each character gives their good reasons not to take action, the magnitude of the task before the Hero becomes more apparent.

In *The Firm*, when the FBI tells Mitch his firm works for the Mafia and has murdered every lawyer who tried to leave, Mitch refuses to break his lawyer-client confidentiality oath, get himself disbarred, and live in the witness protection program for the rest of his life. He refuses, but continuing to work with the firm isn't an option either.

The refusal can also be made by another character, which has the effect of emphasizing the Hero's risk, without portraying him as a Coward. The voice of common sense from a sidekick can point out the risks, dangers and blatant stupidity of the act. In *The Incredibles*, Mr. Incredible's wife, Elastigirl, and friend, Frozone, keep pointing out to Mr. Incredible that his inclination to be a superhero must be suppressed.

Stage Four: Meeting with the Guide

Meeting with the Guide is a cross-over between the path of the Hero and either the Mentor or the Crone. The Mentor's path is to release his power to a worthy recipient. He hopes their union will result in a benefit to future generations that will be his legacy. The Crone's power is to support people's transformation, by creating chaos or supplying a bit of magic.

The Mentor and the Crone guide the Hero in several ways. The Mentor focuses on the requirements to save the village. He prepares the Hero for the task ahead with training, wisdom, knowledge, and gifts. The Crone uses her magic to keep the Hero alive and encourage his personal transformation. She nudges the Hero forward when the Coward archetype has a hold on him. She also creates the environment for him to tame his fear emotion and stand as an individual.

PREPARES THE HERO FOR THE TASK

Over the Mentor's lifetime of being out in the world he has accumulated items of value and developed the skills to use them. He has knowledge and wisdom from his journeys that will increase the Hero's chances of success. The Mentor passes these on to the Hero and makes the Hero greater than he would be on his own. He is the coach, the boss or the military leader who prepares the Hero for the **Final Battle**.

In *The Matrix*, Morpheus phones Neo as he awakens from his dream and asks Neo if he would like to meet. He offers Neo a pill that will let him think whatever he wants, and a pill that will reveal the truth to him. Neo chooses the truth and is horrified to learn he is living in 2199. His entire world is a neural interactive simulator and in reality he is an energy cell for Artificial Intelligence. Morpheus tells Neo they are looking for the one who can save the human race and he believes Neo is that man.

The Mentor is not always a kindly character. In *Alien*, the Mentor is a computer named Mother. This Mentor is strictly offering knowledge. In *The Firm*, Avery provides Mitch with the information he needs to survive in the firm including how far to bend the law and the rules of the firm before they will break. Avery also hits on Mitch's wife. Mitch is unwittingly playing in a dangerous game and Avery reveals the dangers to him and ends Mitch's naiveté.

An Officer and a Gentleman and *Private Benjamin* have military leaders who fill the Guide role by providing the training and mental toughness needed by the Hero for the challenge ahead. The Guide knows what the Hero needs based on his life experience.

NUDGES THE HERO FORWARD

The Crone gives the Hero the perspective and encouragement needed to move forward when the Coward archetype has a grip on him. In *The Insider*, when Jeff Wiegand is faced with keeping his severance package or stopping the cigarette company from using cigarettes as nicotine delivery systems, he is afraid for himself and for his family. The *60 Minutes* producer, Lowell Bergman, tells Jeff he is important and has an opportunity to make a difference. It is this support and perspective that gives Jeff the courage to take the tough journey.

Colonel Coetzee (*Blood Diamond*) has used Danny to his advantage but he also sees who Danny is. Coetzee tells Danny that he is a part of the red soil of Africa and will never leave. This wisdom allows Danny to make good decisions when death is imminent.

The Crone creates chaos in the Hero's life that propels him on his journey regardless of the Coward archetype's objections. The Crone in *The Wizard of Oz*, the good witch Glinda, gives Dorothy the red slippers which mark her as the girl who killed the Wicked Witch of the West's sister and sends the witch after her. This launches Dorothy into facing her fear of death when she finally faces the witch.

Obi-Wan Kenobi and Morpheus are playing the Crone, in *Star Wars* and *The Matrix* respectively, when they sacrifices themselves in battle, giving the Heroes the drive to overcome their complex and complete the mission. In *Alien*, Ash plays the Crone when he allows the infected crew member on board. He challenges Ripley to step up to the plate and fill her leadership role. Her initial failure to take charge endangers the crew and warns her not to make that mistake again.

KEEPS THE HERO ALIVE

In the early stages the Crone uses her magic to keep the Hero alive by protecting a space in which the Hero can grow. When Obi-Wan Kenobi and Luke first enter the space port of Mos Eisley, they are stopped by soldiers looking for R2D2. Luke's story could have ended right there, but Obi-Wan Kenobi uses his magic to hold back evil long enough for Luke to grow into his destiny.

In *Willow*, the Crone, Fin Raziel, uses her magic to resurrect their soldiers when Bavmorda has turned them into swine. She and Willow face the evil queen Bavmorda, tricking her into letting Willow and the soldiers into the castle. Fin Raziel keeps Willow's mission alive and prepares Willow to face Bavmorda alone in the **Final Battle**.

Stage Five: Crossing the First Threshold

By this point in the story, any barrier the Hero felt to accepting the adventure is outweighed or removed, and the Hero selflessly commits to the adventure for the good of his village. The tipping point may have been a further upset or offense to the order of the village, or chaos created by the Crone. However it happens, the decision to go is often made by crossing an actual threshold. At this juncture, there is no turning back for the Hero until the village has been saved.

In *Alien*, once Ash opens the hatch, allowing the infected crew to cross the threshold into the main ship, Ripley identifies Ash as a problem. The alien has entered the ship and endangers the entire crew. The crew is launched on the journey of learning the real agenda of the commercial spaceship.

In *Blood Diamond*, Danny and Solomon have escaped gunfire and are moving towards Solomon's son, Dia, and the diamond, when they are stopped at a checkpoint. The only way to pass is to convince Maddy to tell the guards they are with the press. To do this, Danny gives Maddy some of the information she wants and seals his fate. If he doesn't get the diamond, he has to stay in Africa, and the diamond consortium will have Danny killed.

Crossing the First Threshold is often portrayed symbolically. Thresholds are liminal zones that mark the point of transition. They are doorways, archways, or portals from one world to another. Joan Wilder steps on a bus in Colombia, pursued by a military butcher and the kidnappers, launching her adventure in *Romancing the Stone*; Jason enters a bank vault past guards and lock systems and makes contact with his past identity (*The Bourne Identity*); the Hero enters a bar (*Unforgiven*, *Star Wars*, *Pirates of the Caribbean*) and Marty jumps into the car (*Back to the Future*).

These thresholds are often flanked by guardians tasked with making sure pretenders don't get in. In *Some Like It Hot*, Joe and Gerry walk the length of the train dressed as dames for the first time, not sure if they are believable. They step up onto the train with the two managers guarding the entrance, asking questions about their validity. With a bunch of lies and a lot of nerve, the boys get on the train.

The final push to **Crossing the First Threshold** comes when the consequence of inaction would be death or worse. The greater value of the metaphoric womb, be it the village, a loved one, or goodness and nurturance, makes facing death bearable. The question is, when the Hero is cut off from the safety of the village, will he return a Hero or a Coward, or will he return at all?

Stage Six: Test, Allies, Enemies

During **Tests, Allies, Enemies** the Hero gathers his resources. No longer surrounded by the comforts of home, the Hero feels how big the world is and his physical vulnerability. It is the zone in which he can develop his skills, bravery and ruggedness.

TESTS

The Hero needs to be able to take care of himself and handle pain and loneliness. He develops this skill and ruggedness through a series of tests. These tests demonstrate his character and his weakness, and build tension as to whether he has what it takes to save the village.

In *Blood Diamond,* Danny tells Solomon that he can get him through war-torn Sierra Leone, back to the site where the diamond is hidden and reunite him with his wife, daughter, and son. Danny proves himself able to fulfill these commitments by getting Solomon out of a skirmish when they meet, and by locating his wife and daughter in a camp. However, Dia is still to be found.

Often the Hero fails these early tests, which highlight his weakness, what he must learn, or the magnitude of the task. In *The Firm,* Mitch is tested in the Cayman Islands when he meets the Mafia clients and proves his skill as a negotiator. Later, he fails the test of his character when he takes the bait of a prostitute hired by the firm. Now the firm can blackmail Mitch to keep him loyal to them. Jason (*The Bourne Identity*) is constantly tested as a person with amnesia and by a series of Treadstone agents sent to kill him. He proves to be a highly skilled killer.

ALLIES

The Hero is learning he can stand on his own. He is also selflessly taking on a mission for the good of a group. He amasses masculine power by gathering allies to join in the mission to assert their will over evil. Therefore, the allies are not people from his childhood but strangers he has met on his journey. The Hero may embark on his journey with a friend but they form a composite protagonist or dual protagonists and together they meet strangers and form a new group.

In *Princess Bride*, Westley chases Buttercup's captors and climbs the Cliff of Insanity. At the top he meets the Spaniard who has studied swordsmanship all his life in order to someday kill the six-fingered man who murdered his father. The two duel and develop a mutual respect until Westley knocks the Spaniard out. Westley next meets the Giant and out-wrestles him, leaving him alive. Finally Westley meets the Sicilian who is evil and outsmarts him, leaving the Sicilian dead. When the Spaniard discovers the six-fingered man is the Prince's henchman, the Spaniard, Westley and the Giant band together as allies to storm the castle.

The Virgin is often an ally to the Hero. Jenny is seeking to make a place for herself in the Beverly Hills' art world when her childhood friend Axel Foley comes to town and together they avenge the death of their friend (*Beverly Hills Cop*). The whores in *Unforgiven* provide information and shelter that enables William Munny to right the wrong done to them. In *Romancing the Stone*, Jack (playing the Virgin) is trying to fulfill his dream of owning a sailboat when he meets Joan and joins her heroic mission to save her sister.

It is not necessary for the allies to be friends. They share a common goal or the ally pushes the Hero towards what he must do. For example, in *The Firm*, Mitch doesn't like the FBI agent or trust him, but they have a common goal of bringing down the law firm that is working for the Mafia and murdering partners. Mitch is able to use the FBI agent to get himself and Abby out of the mess they are in.

The tests help the Hero identify his allies. When the Hero's back is against the wall, people with the same enemy or purpose join his side. In *Willow,* Willow and Madmartigan are at cross-purposes until the baby is threatened by the queen's soldiers. Suddenly they have a common purpose: to get the baby Elora to safety. Through the test of escaping the queen's soldiers, Willow sees that Madmartigan truly is a great warrior and Madmartigan sees that Willow is brave and true to his purpose and they become allies.

ENEMIES

During **Tests, Allies, Enemies** the Hero often has a first introduction to the villain's character and power. In *Beverly Hills Cop,* Axel comes to Beverly Hills to avenge the murder of his friend, and walks straight into the office of his prime suspect. The man has him thrown out of the building through a plate-glass wall and arrested for disturbing the peace. This is one powerful guy in Los Angeles.

The villain is a representation of the boundary between mortality and immortality. He recklessly holds the lives of others in his hands, emphasizing their human frailty, while his own powers seem to make him immortal. Even children's stories have villains so evil they want to kill puppies to make a coat (*101 Dalmatians*), or kill women and children to gain domination over China (*Mulan*). The villains are excessively self-focused and use power to dominate others, providing a high contrast to the Hero, who selflessly risks his life for his village. He either has no empathy for others, or actively seeks to inflict pain because of a complex. The Hero is focused on the benevolent use of power in the hands of a group. In this battle of mythic proportions to assert power, the villain is godlike as the Hero challenges his domain and explores the limits of his mortality. The more evil the villain is, the braver the Hero is able to be.

Stage Seven: Preparations

Once the Hero has amassed a group of allies, they need to get information or some object that will increase their chances of success in the **Final Battle**. They begin by making a plan to infiltrate the villain's inner sanctum. There is a moment of calm while the Hero and his allies plan and bond as a group. The operation is laid out, dangers are highlighted, and the significance of the mission is explained. The allies clean their weapons, dress for battle, or sit around the campfire or in a bar and share a moment of camaraderie.

The villain's lair may be the location of a treasure, the hiding place of a kidnapped person, or the secret headquarters of the villain's operations. The object is to get in and get out, and be wiser for the effort. There is tension in the air. Everyone is aware that once they enter the villain's inner sanctum they will become known to the enemy and the target of his wrath.

In *Alien,* the crew sits around the breakfast table and assesses their situation. They determine the alien is in the duct system and make a plan for trapping and expelling it. In *Romancing the Stone,* Jack and Joan find an abandoned airplane and take shelter. In this quiet moment, they make a plan to follow the map to get the stone and use it to bargain for the release of Joan's sister.

Stage Eight: Crisis

The **Crisis** is the first major confrontation with the antagonist. The villain's power is revealed and the Hero gets a good taste of fear as he barely escapes with his life. This is sometimes known as the false death and comes as a foreshadowing of the impending challenge to death in the **Final Battle**.

When the Hero enters the villain's lair, it is a dark, womb-like place, and the question hangs heavy in the air, "Will I survive getting out of here?" Often allies are eliminated like cattle in a slaughterhouse to emphasize death's proximity. In this encounter between the Hero and evil, the Hero just barely survives through luck or help from others, but he learns he can face death and walk away. He has successfully expanded the boundaries of his mortality and is ready to push them even farther.

In *Star Wars*, Luke Skywalker and his crew are sucked into the Death Star when they are looking to rescue Princess Leia. They find and release her but their attempt to escape lands them in the trash compacter with the walls closing in. Suddenly, C-3PO's voice comes over the communication device and he shuts down the trash compactor. The allies escape with their lives and feel elated.

The **Crisis** in *Unforgiven* occurs when William Munny arrives in town and meets the villain, Little Bill, who beats him brutally for carrying a firearm. Hanging on the edge of death he is nursed back to life by the whores. Suddenly William is aware of how amazing it is to be alive, which he hasn't felt since his wife died. Jack (*Titanic*), is accused of stealing the gemstone that is planted on him by Rose's fiancé. Jack finds himself in a power struggle where social status is equated with credibility, and he has none. He is chained to a pole in the lower deck as the ship starts to go down, all his dreams about to drown, when Rose finds him and they escape. Jack now knows his purpose in life is to save Rose.

Stage Nine: Reward

The Hero gains inspiration and information from the **Crisis** that gives him the edge when he again faces evil. He has a renewed drive to ensure that evil no longer threatens the safety of his village. The Hero grabs the sword, the potion, the hostage, the information, or his new self-realization as his **Reward**, and takes a moment to celebrate. On a personal note, the weight of his complex has lifted and he feels lighter.

SEIZES THE SWORD

The **Reward** can be something tangible, such as the diamond in *Blood Diamond*, that becomes pivotal in the Hero's eventual success. The diamond gives Solomon the means to trap the diamond traders and work to end violence in his country. It also provides the means for Solomon to buy safe passage for his family. Taking the diamond from the colonel and killing him allows Danny to avenge the wrongs done to him as a child and eventually act selflessly for the betterment of his country.

The broom and the slippers in *The Wizard of Oz* are "swords" for Dorothy. Delivering the broom requires the wizard to put power back in the hands of the individuals. The slippers, with the knowledge that there is no place like home, hold the magic to reverse Dorothy's journey.

In *The Bourne Identity*, Jason kills a Treadstone agent and confiscates his cell phone. Now Jason has the ability to contact the head of Treadstone, get information, and set up a meeting. The cell phone becomes his tangible **Reward**.

A NEW REALIZATION

A new realization can enhance the Hero's ability to defeat the villain and is therefore his **Reward**. This may be letting go of a belief that was holding the Hero back. In *The Matrix*, Neo is not the One because he doesn't believe in himself. Faced with Morpheus's certain death, Neo suddenly believes he can bring Morpheus back and he does. This causes him to turn and face the Agent rather than run when they come face to face. Neo has let go of the belief that he is nobody and started to believe he is the One, which is his **Reward**.

In the **Reward**, John and Billy decide to join Axel and rescue Jenny (*Beverly Hills Cop*). They risk their lives and careers for him because they are working as a team.

Through the **Crisis** the Hero faces death and in that moment he faces his complex and lets it go. Jack transcends the stigma of his humble beginnings and knows his value to Rose (*Titanic*), Danny stops being the child who has to slip under the radar and becomes the adult who can stand up to the colonel and save Dia from what was once his fate (*Blood Diamond*).

NEW INFORMATION

Information can also be the **Reward** for surviving the **Crisis**. In *The Firm*, Mitch is caught between the FBI, the firm, and the Mafia until he learns the firm has been overbilling and using the federal mail system to deliver their invoices. This is a crime punishable by jail time and a fine for each offense. Now Mitch has the means to keep his career and put the partners in jail for many years. The **Reward** is seeing a way out of his predicament.

In *Alien*, Ripley discovers Ash was a robot planted by the company to bring back an alien to be sold as a military weapon, even at the expense of the crew. Once she discovers the enemy within and eliminates it, Ripley can focus on killing the alien. This discovery is her **Reward**.

CELEBRATION OF BEING ALIVE

The **Reward** is also a moment to celebrate being alive. A sex scene with the Virgin is often a metaphor for this joy in having a living, breathing body. In this moment the internal and the external journey to know self are melded. This moment occurs in *An Officer and a Gentleman* when Zack and Paula make love. *Raiders of the Lost Ark* also includes a scene of reward when Marion kisses Indiana's bruises and cuts. In *The Last Samurai*, Taka undresses and dresses Captain Nathan Algren in the clothes of a revered samurai in a sensual scene. After years of wishing he were dead, Nathan finds beauty in every breath.

Romance may inspire the Hero to adventure but it is not necessary for the Hero to find everlasting love on his journey. When the love interest is a Virgin she is a symbol of what is good and worth fighting for. The challenge of the Hero is to prove he can stand on his own. He is not trying to join his life with another.

Stage Ten: The Road Back

The Hero has faced death and survived. He has gained some kind of reward from this experience and armed with this knowledge, realization, or sword, the Hero looks to secure the future of the village. He knows he must face death again, but this time he must do more than just survive. He needs the skill, cunning, and strength to assert his will over the will of the villain. Youth is confronting the elder and taking up his power. "Kill the King! Kill the King! Long live the King!" is the ancient chant that describes this transition from the old king to the new, more virile king.

Neo is unable to kill Agent Smith so he runs (*The Matrix*). Agent Smith catches up with him and shoots Neo dead. But Trinity won't accept Neo's death. She is no longer afraid to tell Neo she loves him and, according to the Oracle, that makes him the One. Neo comes back to life. He discovers his death was an illusion that he can overcome with love.

The Road Back is complicated by a seemingly impossible series of obstacles heaped onto the Hero. The obstacles may be manifest in many ways. If the villain escapes, the Hero is in a race against time to find and stop the villain before he achieves his plan of mass destruction. There may be a chase scene, a shoot-out or a further insult to the village. Every conceivable danger, complication or hardship is placed before the Hero. If the Hero has a morbid fear of snakes, there will be a snake pit to be crossed.

In *Beverly Hills Cop*, Axel enters the stronghold of the villain, his gated home crawling with armed guards and surveillance cameras, to rescue his friend. The Los Angeles cops arrive for support and together they scale the wall. Axel moves around the property looking for the "king" as numerous gunmen shoot at him.

In *Blood Diamond*, Danny, Solomon, and Dia flee with RUF soldiers in hot pursuit. They must climb the mountain to the plateau where the plane will land at the appointed time. It will not wait. Wounded, Danny realizes he is slowing them down. The soldiers are gaining on them but they can't slow the soldiers down with gunfire and climb. Solomon tries to carry Danny but they are still too slow. All these events are building the tension as the Hero moves towards the Final Battle.

Stage Eleven: The Final Battle

In the face of impossible odds and almost certain death, the Hero rises to his potential in the **Final Battle**, which is the climax of the movie. Previously the Hero came to the realization that he can recover from near-death. Now the Hero proves his transformation has become a part of him. The **Final Battle** may come in the form of a one-on-one battle between the Hero and the villain, an executed plan by the allies, or a choice. The story may employ one, two, or all of these methods. The Hero risks death in a selfless act and the village is made secure again. As in myths, the Hero may even die in the **Final Battle**, having successfully proven himself or failed in a tragic ending.

ONE LAST BATTLE

In the **Final Battle**, the Hero's selfless use of power is up against the villain or Tyrant's, who wields his power for personal gain. These two ideologies, embodied by the Hero and the villain, each have a following. When the two warring factions meet on the battlefield, the Hero and the villain always find each other and battle for supremacy.

In *Unforgiven*, William guns down a few cowboys and then faces Little Bill, determined to avenge the death of his friend and end the oppressive use of power in town. Little Bill is fighting in the name of brutal, patriarchal rule. William kills Little Bill, and the rest of the cowboys scatter. He steps out into the street, threatening to kill anyone, and their loved one, who takes a shot at him. He commands them to treat the whores well and to give

Ned a decent burial or he will come back. The power of William Munny's persona has exceeded his human potential and he is using it for good.

After shooting his way past the guards with Billy and John, Axel has a bloody shoot-out with the villain in *Beverly Hills Cop*. In *Alien*, Ripley and the remaining crew undergo a **Final Battle** with the alien to eject it into space. The other crew members are killed and Ripley escapes in the space shuttle only to find the alien is on board with her. She goes one on one with the alien and ejects it into space. Joan and Jack have a **Final Battle** with Zolo in *Romancing the Stone*, in which Joan feeds Zolo to the crocodiles, and Jack jumps into the water to recover the stone. In each of these cases, the climax occurs when the Hero and the villain fight it out directly and the Hero proves his worth.

An Executed Plan

The **Final Battle** may also occur as a plan that must be correctly executed for the success of the allies. Rather than entering into a face-to-face battle, the Hero and his forces work to remove the villain's power, possibly in the form of money, reputation, or a weapon.

In *Star Wars*, the allies know that a single bomb in a precise weak spot could trigger a chain reaction that would destroy the Death Star. The enemy becomes aware of the allies' plan and sends fighter jets to shoot them out of the sky. Luke is the last surviving pilot and, while heavily under fire, he must hit the tiny target and execute the plan. Trusting the force within him, Luke makes the impossible shot that destroys the Death Star.

In *The Firm*, Mitch devises a plan whereby he can obtain the information he needs to blackmail the Mafia into not killing him, and the records he needs to facilitate the FBI sending the firm partners to jail for a long time. He does this while preserving his ability to practice law and live outside the witness protection program. Together, Mitch, Abbey and Tammy execute the plan.

A CHOICE

Making the right choice can also defeat evil in the **Final Battle**. Detective John Book makes a choice for non-violence in the climax of *Witness*, showing his transformation to a man who understands the ways of the Amish people. His old self has been allowed to die and a new man has risen. Evil, in the form of the belief that violence is the only way to solve problems, is defeated.

In *Blood Diamond*, Danny faces his demons, which have made him focus on helping himself. Danny makes a choice to get Dia out of Sierra Leone to become a doctor, and to expose the diamond traders and end the financing of bloody battles driven by greed. He stays behind to hold off the soldiers and makes a phone call to arrange for the success of Dia's future. It is a quiet climax with the heart-wrenching acceptance of the higher purpose of the Hero.

Similarly, in *Thelma and Louise*, both women face the choice of going to prison, where Louise knows only too well the humiliations they will be subjected to, or taking control of their lives and driving over the cliff. This decision is a form of asserting one's will against the will of others and a means of defeating evil in the **Final Battle**, sometimes at the expense of the Hero's life.

Stage Twelve: Return with the Elixir

The Hero has thwarted the impending threat to the village. The village is now safe, the wrong has been righted, order has been restored, or the source of evil has been removed. The Hero **Returns with the Elixir**, which secures the future safety of the village. The elixir may be something tangible, such as a magic sword that always wins battles and thereby keeps invaders at bay. Alternatively, it may be a form of knowledge, namely, the Hero has learned he can exist outside the womb and can therefore return and take his place as the Lover/King. When the Hero returns to his village, there is often a celebration and recognition of the transformation which has occurred in the Hero.

In *Alien*, Ripley speaks into the ship's log as she returns to Earth, the sole survivor of the mission. She brings back the wisdom that commercial ships sent into space with a financial priority are a threat to the survival of mankind. In *Romancing the Stone*, Jack shows up in Joan's life with a sailboat and a pair of crocodile boots. Joan learns she was right to trust Jack and has found her true love in a real man rather than a fantasy. In *Willow*, the prophecy has come true and a loving king and queen (Madmartigan and Sorsha) will raise the baby Elora to someday rule the kingdom. Willow is granted wizard status when he returns home as he has found the power within him. His return is celebrated by his family and his village.

In the end, the Hero has successfully overcome his fear of death and his Mother Complex. He no longer needs to be taken care of by his village because he owns his power and his ability to exist in the world. The Hero returns to the village with a new role, one of providing ongoing protection and stability.

Hero Film Summaries

The following film summaries track an entire Hero's journey through the beats of the archetypal structure. The numbers in brackets indicate the stages of the Hero's journey as described above.

Alien

Ripley and six other crew members are on the commercial starship *Nostromo* in the year 2037, heading back to earth in their sleeping pods (1). They are awakened early by the ship's control system, Mother, to investigate a nearby planet (2). Exploring the terrain, they come across a nest of large eggs and an alien life form sucks onto crew member Cain. Ripley, the acting captain onboard, refuses to allow the crew members out of the holding chamber until they are decontaminated (3), but the science officer, Ash, overrides her and lets them in (5). Ripley questions Ash about the alien and grows to distrust him. She conferences with Captain Dallas and finds out Ash was a last-minute replacement on this mission (6). Cain explodes and an alien is released into the air duct system (7). Captain Dallas enters the ducts with a torch, attempting to corral the alien to a place where it can be ejected. Dallas is killed and Ripley takes over the mission (6). Mother informs Ripley (4) that Ash has orders to bring back an alien life form for military sales and the crew is considered expendable (9). Ash attacks Ripley but she is saved by the technical crew (8). Ripley lashes back at Ash and discovers Ash is a computer that was working against them to bring back the alien (9). Ripley and the two remaining crew members make a plan to retreat to the shuttle and destroy the spaceship, with the alien on board (10). The two crew members are killed trying to get enough air tanks to make the journey in the shuttle (10). Ripley blasts off in the shuttle and destroys the spaceship only to find the alien is on the shuttle (10). In a final battle, Ripley ejects the alien (11) and returns to Earth with the evidence that commercial ships sent into space with a financial priority are a threat to mankind's survival (12).

Alien scores twelve out of twelve.

Beverly Hills Cop

Detroit cop Axel Foley, who grew up poor and narrowly escaped juvenile detention for car theft, is a clever cop but a renegade (1). His childhood friend, Mikey, who started his life of crime as a juvenile, suddenly shows up with a fortune in bonds and offers to cut Axel in (2). Axel is uncomfortable letting down his friend but won't risk his career as a cop (3). Two thugs, one named Zack, show up, knock out Axel and kill Mikey. Axel is warned by his police chief that he is a good cop but doesn't work as a team player (4), and if Axel gets involved in the murder investigation, he will lose his job (3). Axel takes a vacation and heads to Beverly Hills to track down the source of the bonds. Axel learns from Jenny, another friend from the old neighborhood (6), that Mikey worked for her boss, an art dealer named Victor Maitland. Axel marches into Victor's office and announces his intention to find Mikey's killer (6). Axel is removed from the building, thrown through a glass wall, and arrested for disturbing the peace (6, 5). Axel meets the Los Angeles police, who are working as a team, loyal to their chief (6). Axel makes friends with detectives Billy and John and shares what he has learned about Victor's smuggling operation (6, 7). With Jenny's help, Axel enters the warehouse to get evidence of Victor's drug smuggling while Billy waits outside (7). Victor discovers them and kidnaps Jenny, leaving Zack and two thugs to kill Axel (8). Zack taunts Axel, revealing he killed Mikey. Billy decides to break procedure and go in after Axel (9). They escape (8) and go after Jenny at Victor's mansion (10). John decides to support Axel and calls for back-up before entering the grounds with Billy and Axel (9). They shoot their way through guards until Axel has a final showdown with Victor and kills him, saving Jenny (11). The police chief spins a story to explain the break from procedure to his superiors and Axel is able to return to Detroit a hero, having learned the importance of being a team player (12).

Beverly Hills Cop scores twelve out of twelve.

Blood Diamond

A fisherman named Solomon and his loving family live in Sierra Leone in 1999 (1). His son, Dia, is going to be a doctor someday (1). Danny Archer is a white Rhodesian who smuggles diamonds and deals in guns for a living (1). During the brutal civil war, a rebel attack splits up Solomon's family and sends Solomon to a diamond mine as a laborer and Dia to a child-soldier training camp (2). During a raid on the mine, Solomon finds a large diamond, and, risking death, he manages to bury it before being taken to jail (2). But a guard knows Solomon has hidden a diamond and rumors ripple through the jail (6). Danny happens to be in jail and hears of the diamond (2). He attaches himself to Solomon, who wants nothing to do with Danny (3). Danny meets Maddy, a journalist, at a resort and she challenges him to expose the diamond dealers and make a difference in the Sierra Leone war (2). Danny tells her, "Piss off. I like to get kissed before I get fucked" (3). Danny meets with his old army colonel, who taught him the diamond-smuggling game, and the colonel tries to trap Danny into working for him again. The colonel tells Danny the soil is red from their blood and Danny will never leave (4). Danny has a plan to get enough money to escape Africa and convinces Solomon to split the diamond if Danny reunites Solomon's family. They are stopped at a blockade and Danny decides to give Maddy information on the diamond traders in exchange for help finding Solomon's son, including passes to travel as journalists (5). There is no turning back for Danny now (5). Danny and Maddy bring Solomon to his wife and daughter, only to find Dia was taken by the rebels (6). They travel to the Komo Mine, dodging RUF and local militia, and find Dia (7). Solomon risks all to take Dia away but Dia has been brainwashed by the rebels and refuses to go. Solomon is captured (8). Danny calls in the colonel who leads an air raid on the camp, and in the massacre Danny saves Dia. The colonel lands and forces Danny and Solomon to lead him to the diamond at gunpoint (8). They scuffle and Danny kills the colonel and retrieves the diamond (9). Dia gets a gun and turns it on Danny (8). Solomon talks Dia into remembering he is a good boy who will someday be a doctor (9). As soldiers close in, Dia, Solomon, and Danny climb the valley to meet the airplane in the plateau, but Danny is wounded (10). Solomon carries him for a while but Danny can see they won't make it (10). Danny gives Solomon the diamond and sends Solomon and Dia to the plane while he holds off the soldiers (11). Danny sees the important thing is for boys like Dia to grow up and be doctors and create a new vision for Sierra Leone (11). As the plane takes off, Danny calls Maddy and gives her information to help Solomon tell the world how the diamonds are being smuggled to fund the Sierra Leone war (11). Danny dies with the red soil of Africa in his bloody hand. Solomon and Maddy expose the diamond industry (11), enabling Sierra Leone to become the paradise it once was (12).

Blood Diamond scores twelve out of twelve.

The Bourne Identity

A man is found floating in the Mediterranean with two bullet holes in his back and a capsule under his skin with a Swiss bank number (1). He has amnesia and must find out who the hell he is (2). When challenged, he is a fighting machine, cool and clever (1). He goes to the Swiss bank and gets the box. There is money, lots of it, a passport that tells him he is Jason Bourne, multiple other identities, and a gun. A man working for the CIA is alerted that Jason Bourne has shown up at the bank, and the mission to kill Jason is launched (5). Jason defeats the entire American Embassy security force and convinces Marie, a woman trying to get a visa and in need of money, to give him a ride to Paris, where he apparently has an apartment (6). Three special CIA agents of the Treadstone project are activated to kill Jason (6). Jason kills one of them in his apartment leaving Maria traumatized (6). Information suggests an exiled African leader, Wambossi, knows Jason's identity. When Jason and Marie arrive at Wambossi's residence, Wambossi has been assassinated. Jason learns from the newspaper that he is an assassin who failed his mission and ended up in the ocean (1). Now Jason must get Marie to safety and run alone (7). They go to Marie's friend Emon's country home, hoping it will be empty, when Emon shows up with his two kids and a dog (7). They stay the night and Jason is compelled to watch over the kids. Bits of memory come back and he doesn't want to know who he is any more (3). Jason asks Marie if she will disappear with him (3). In the morning the dog is missing. Jason tells everyone to get into the basement and hunts down the agent who is hunting him (5, 8). Jason kills the agent after learning they are fellow Treadstone agents (8, 9). Jason takes the agent's cell phone (9) and makes contact with Treadstone. Jason gives Marie most of the money and tells her to make a life for herself. He sets up a meeting and tracks the Treadstone unit leader back to Paris headquarters (10). In a confrontation, Jason's memory comes flooding back to him. He couldn't complete his mission because there were children in the room. Jason's conscience overrode his training as an assassin (11). He declares he is on his own side now and will track down and kill anyone who comes after him. The third agent kills the Treadstone unit leader. Jason finds Marie running a remote shop and they are happy (12).

The Bourne Identity scores twelve out of twelve.

The Firm

Harvard law school graduate Mitch McTeer is being courted by every major law firm in the States. With his loving, well-bred wife Abby at his side, Mitch feels he can finally leave behind the poverty of his childhood and the social stigma of a divorced mother with a series of loser boyfriends and a brother in jail (1). The law firm Bendini Lambert and Lock want Mitch, no matter what the cost (2), but after the introductory visit to Memphis, Abby finds their policies disturbing (3). But this is Mitch's dream of the good life, so they take the job (5). Avery Toller, a tax lawyer, is assigned as Mitch's mentor, letting him know just how far he can bend the rules of law and the firm (4). The company has Mitch's house and car bugged, and watches how suspicious Mitch gets when two lawyers from the firm die (6). Mitch is taken to the Cayman Islands and proves his ability to work with difficult clients (6). There is mention of an ominous Chicago connection, about whom Avery doesn't want to talk (6). Mitch meets the owner of the boat that exploded with the deceased partners on it and learns there were two other men on board who were never reported: an albino and a stocky Italian (6). The firm baits Mitch with a prostitute who shares his desire for material status and he can't resist her (6), giving the firm blackmail power over Mitch. When Mitch finds a closet full of files from all the deceased partners of the firm, he knows he is in trouble, and goes to visit his brother, Ray, in jail (7). Ray hooks him up with a private detective who asks some questions and is killed by the albino and Italian (6). The detective's secretary/lover, Tammy, informs Mitch of what happened and agrees to help him (6, 7). The FBI approach Mitch to become an informant against the firm, which is involved in laundering Mafia money. Mitch refuses because he would be disbarred for breaking the client-lawyer confidentiality oath and spend the rest of his and Abby's life in the witness protection program (3). Mitch recognizes the firm probably saw him be approached, and goes right to the partners and tells them the FBI wants the "secret files" (8). Mitch now knows how the firm is trapping him and is determined to outsmart them when he realizes they have been overbilling through the federal mail system (9). Mitch and Tammy steal and start copying files that indicate the firm has been overbilling and mailing the bills, making it a federal offence punishable by $10,000 in fines and three to five years in prison for each offence (10). Tammy and Abby copy the files on the Mafia dealings in the Cayman Islands. The albino and the firm security expert come after Mitch and are killed (10). Mitch gives the FBI the illegal billing information that will put the firm's partners in jail. Mitch meets with the Mafia headmen and explains that as long as he is alive he is bound by client-lawyer confidentiality not to share the information he has (11). Mitch has gotten his life back and rediscovered his passion for the law (12). He also realizes money is not as important as his love for his wife (12).

The Firm scores twelve out of twelve.

The Matrix

Thomas Anderson is a program writer for a respectable software company in 1999. He lives alone in a tiny apartment dominated by computer equipment where he goes by the name Neo and sells illegal software (1). A message appears on his computer to follow the white rabbit and it takes Neo to a club where he meets Trinity, an infamous software hacker (5). She tells him she knows all about him and the feeling he has that he is in a dream. Trinity tells Neo he is in danger and Agents are watching him (2). The next day Agents come to Neo's office. Morpheus phones him and tries to guide his escape but when faced with climbing outside onto the scaffolding Neo prefers to be arrested (3). Agents implant Neo with a bug and he awakens from a dream (5). Morpheus phones and offers to meet with Neo (4). Morpheus acknowledges the feeling Neo has that something is wrong but he can't figure it out. He offers Neo a blue pill if he wants to believe whatever he wants or a red pill to know the truth. Neo takes the red pill (5). Morpheus tells Neo it is really 2199. After Artificial Intelligence was created there was a battle for control and now humans are battery cells for machines controlled by an illusion (5). Neo wakes up in a gooey pod with electrical attachments on his body. He is identified as defective by the machine and flushed. Morpheus picks him up in his spaceship and begins Neo's training (5). Neo learns martial arts and frees his mind to bend the laws of nature such as gravity and perform superhuman feats (6). Morpheus believes they will all be saved by the One. He believes Neo is the One (7). He takes Neo to the Oracle who asks Neo if he thinks he is the One. Neo says no. The Oracle tells him he is not the One but will have to choose between his life and Morpheus's because Morpheus will sacrifice himself to save Neo. Returning to the spaceship they are trapped by Agents because one of their members, Cypher, has betrayed them in order to go back to the illusion (8). They kill the traitor among them but when Neo returns to the ship he finds the Agents are bending Morpheus's brain to learn the location of Zion, the last community of humans. Morpheus must be killed to protect the information. Neo stops them because he suddenly knows what he can do. He may not be the One but he believes he can bring Morpheus back (10). Neo and Trinity boldly enter the Agent's building, shoot it up and rescue Morpheus (10). Neo is left behind and faces Agent Smith rather than run. He is beginning to believe he is the One who can beat the Agents (9). Neo beats him but Agent Smith just comes back and shoots Neo dead (8). Disbelieving what has happened, Trinity tells Neo he can't be dead because she loves him and, according to the Oracle, that makes him the One. Neo realizes his death was an illusion he can choose not to accept and he comes back to life for love (9). He sees Agent Smith is simply a matrix of numbers and he knows how to defeat him (11). Agent Smith explodes and the other Agents scatter. Neo telepaths to the ship just before it is destroyed by Sentinels. The phone rings and it is Neo sending a message to the people of today: we live with no controls, boundaries, or rules (1). The choice is up to us: depend on machines or live independently within our environment (12).

The Matrix scores twelve out of twelve.

The Princess Bride

Westley, a farm helper who feels the greatest love of all time for the farmer's daughter, Buttercup, (1) must go away to improve his station in life so he can marry Buttercup (2). Westley is reported dead at the hands of the dreaded pirate Roberts, and Buttercup is chosen by Prince Humperdinck as his bride. Buttercup is kidnapped and taken to a land of impossible hardship (3) by the Sicilian, the Spaniard and the Giant. Roberts follows them and climbs the Cliff of Insanity, bests the Spaniard in a sword fight, out-wrestles the Giant and out-smarts the Sicilian (6). Prince Humperdinck is tracking them to appear concerned, while all along it is he who has arranged for Buttercup's kidnapping and

eventual murder to increase his power (6). Roberts reveals himself to Buttercup as her Westley and together they travel through
the Fire Swamps (6), only to be captured at the other end by
Prince Humperdinck. Westley is taken to a torture chamber (the
Pit of Despair), where he is subjected to unimaginable pain until
he dies (8). The Spaniard on a quest to find the six-fingered man
who killed his father is reunited with the Giant, and they realize they must join with Westley to avenge the Spaniard's father's
death (7). They find Westley's body and take him to Miracle
Max, who discovers Westley is only nearly dead, being kept alive
by true love (4). Miracle Max creates a pill that slowly brings
Westley back to life (9). Together they storm the castle to save the
Princess and kill the six-fingered man although Westley's body is
somewhat paralyzed (10). The six-fingered man and the Spaniard
engage is a brutal swordfight. The Spaniard triumphs despite
numerous stab wounds (11). Westley outsmarts the Prince and
rescues Buttercup (11), and they all leap out the window, care-
free in the knowledge that true love endures all (12).

The Princess Bride scores eleven out of twelve. There is no
clear threshold that Westley crosses to mark the commencement
of his journey (5).

Romancing the Stone

Adventure/romance novelist Joan Wilder lives a safe, isolated life,
writing in her apartment with her cat, and dreams of meeting a
man like Jesse, the hero in her novels (1). A package arrives from
Joan's recently deceased brother-in-law, which contains a treasure
map. A dark man in a fedora, Zolo, kills a neighbor and breaks
into Joan's apartment looking for the map. Elaine, Joan's sister,
calls from Colombia and tells Joan she has to bring the map down
to Cartagena to ransom her (2). Joan says she can't go (3), but she
has to go, for her sister's sake. Joan's publisher strongly advises
against it. Joan gets motion-sick, hasn't had her shots, is afraid of
flying, these people killed her brother-in-law (3)! Joan arrives in

Colombia and is directed by Zolo onto the wrong bus, as the kidnapper, Ralph, follows (5). When the bus is damaged, Zolo pulls a gun on Joan to get the map, and Jack, an American adventurer, arrives and scares him away (6). For $375, Jack agrees to help Joan get to a town and the craziness ensues. Zolo brings the militia and shoots at Jack and Joan, the kidnappers follow and try to steal the map and angry locals threaten them until they learn she is *the* Joan Wilder. They are big fans of her novels so they help (6). In the carcass of an old plane crash Jack gets Joan to tell him what this is all about (6) and convinces Joan to try to get the treasure using the map with him and have more to bargain with for her sister (7). Joan decides to trust Jack, and hopes they can keep the stone and buy Jack a sailboat, with the promise that if they have to give up the stone for her sister they will (7). They follow the map and find the stone, only to be held at gunpoint by Ralph, who takes the stone, then encounters the militia (8). Jack and Joan chase after Ralph, recover the stone (9), and fall over a waterfall with Jack, and the stone, landing on one side and Joan on the other (8). Joan is alive but she believes Jack planned this and her sister's life is in peril (10). Joan makes her way back to the village with the map, phones the kidnappers, and arranges to meet (10). Jack doesn't show up. Joan exchanges Elaine for the map, just as Jack shows up with Zolo pointing a gun at him. Zolo wants the stone or he will feed Joan to the crocodiles. Jack brings out the stone and throws it to the crocodile (11). Zolo catches it and a crocodile takes off Zolo's hand with the stone in it (11). Jack grabs the crocodile by the tail. Zolo goes after Joan. Jack releases the crocodile into the water to come to Joan's aid just as Joan pushes Zolo to the crocodiles (11). The police arrive and Jack jumps into the water. Joan goes home and writes her best novel ever, inspired by her love for Jack (12). Jack shows up, wearing crocodile boots, with a sailboat. Joan was right to have trusted him (12).

Romancing the Stone scores eleven out of twelve. There is no **Meeting with the Guide**.

Unforgiven

Ex-gunslinger William Munny buries his wife, whom he wasn't good enough for, and tries to raise their two kids on a pig farm (1). Meanwhile, in the town of Big Whiskey, a whore is stabbed for giggling at the size of a client's member, and the two cowboys who did it are fined six horses, payable to the whorehouse owner. The outraged whores offer one thousand dollars to whoever kills the cowboys (2). A young man, the Schofield Kid, comes to William looking for a killing partner (2), but William explains he "ain't like that" anymore (3). His wife cured him of his wickedness; he's no longer a drunken killer of women and children. But when William hears that the cowboys cut a woman he figures they got a killing coming to them. The pigs are sick and it will be hard to survive the winter, so William decides to catch up with the Schofield Kid (5), even though he can't shoot or mount his horse worth a hill of beans. William rides to his friend Ned's place to get him to come along (5). Ned reminds William that it has been eleven years since he killed anyone, which his deceased wife would not approve of, but agrees the cowboys got it coming (4). Ned, the Kid, and William size each other up (6). William won't drink, which is really impeding his aim and the Kid is in desperate need of eyeglasses, but together they are a team (6). Meanwhile, the sheriff of Big Whiskey, Little Bill, hears of the bounty and creates an ordinance that no guns are allowed in town. When the nasty gunfighter English Bob wears his guns in town, Little Bill beats him to an inch of his life and puts him on an outgoing coach (6). William, Ned and the Kid arrive in town and find the whores to get information (7). In the Big Whiskey Tavern, William is seeing dead people with worms coming out of their heads. Little Bill finds a gun on William and beats him to near-death (8). William admits that he is afraid to die. His fever breaks and William has an epiphany. He is alive. Rather than focusing on the fact that his wife is dead he wants to live his life (9). They go out and kill one of the cowboys (10). It was not easy to do and Ned decides he is no longer a killer. He heads back to Kansas. En route, Ned is caught and beaten to death by Little Bill, while William and the Kid kill the other cowboy (10). When William learns Ned is dead he starts drinking (11). William walks into the tavern full of cowboys who are readying a posse and kills five men plus Little Bill to avenge Ned (11). The rest scatter. Then William walks into the street, exposed, and yells that if anyone shoots at him he will kill them and their wives and kids, and burn their houses, and they are to give Ned a good burial, and never harm the whores (12). No one takes a shot at him. William Munny returns home with the bounty money and moves his kids to California, where they prosper (12).

Unforgiven scores twelve out of twelve.

Willow

Willow lives in his peaceful village along the riverside with his loving wife Kaiya and their two children (1). In the realm of the evil Queen Bavmorda, a baby is born who bears the mark of the one prophesied to bring down her evil reign. A midwife takes pity on the baby Elora, escapes the castle with her, and floats Elora down the river to the place where Willow's children are playing (2). Willow wants to push the baby along the river and pretend they never met (3) but Kaiya takes her in. The queen's soldiers terrorize the village, looking for a baby (2). The village council decides the baby is to be taken to the Dikini crossroads and given to a human (4). Willow and a small crew set out to deliver Elora. They evade Sorsha's search party (Queen Bavmorda's warrior-daughter) and meet Madmartigan caged at the Dikini crossroads. Madmartigan convinces Willow to release him so he can deliver Elora to safety. Brownies capture Elora, and then Willow and his companion and Willow is told that Elora has chosen him (2). Willow and the Brownies decide to take Elora to a castle where the prophecy says she will be raised by a loving king and queen

(5). They are discovered by Sorsha in a tavern, but Madmartigan helps them to escape and Willow and Madmartigan agree to bring Elora to safety together (6). The party finds the sorcerer Fin Raziel, now imprisoned as a weasel, to give her the wand that will return her powers to fight Queen Bavmorda, but they are captured and taken to the Sorsha's camp (7) before Fin Raziel can be turned back into a powerful sorcerer. As they escape, Madmartigan is infected with a love potion and falls in love with Sorsha, nearly causing their recapture (6). Soldiers loyal to Elora join them and they arrive at the castle where a king and queen were to raise Elora. The castle is abandoned. Queen Bavmorda's army approaches and a great battle ensues (8). Elora is captured and taken to Queen Bavmorda's castle (8). Sorsha comes to see that her mother is evil and she loves Madmartigan, and she joins Elora's side (9). The party loyal to Elora travels to the Queen's castle, where Bavmorda turns them all into pigs, except Willow and Fin Raziel (10). Willow turns Fin Raziel into a sorcerer again and Fin Raziel turns the party back into people (10). They trick Queen Bavmorda into opening the castle gates and enter the castle as the Queen prepares for a ritual killing of Elora (10). Willow outsmarts the Queen, while Madmartigan and the loyal warriors defeat the army (11). Willow returns to the village with the threat of Queen Bavmorda's evil rule removed. Sorsha and Madmartigan raise Elora in the castle that was empty, fulfilling the prophesy. Willow has grown in his self-confidence and becomes a wizard (12).

Willow scores twelve out of twelve.

Part 2

Chapter 5

Screenplay Structure

tructure gives a story shape and direction and creates a movie that is engaging, well paced, and emotionally satisfying. Without it, a story wallows in clutter and rambles aimlessly. Archetypal structure has a strong, unconscious impact and invokes the power of symbols and universal themes of transformation.

Generally, a screenplay is 90 to 120 pages long. This is the strongest structural element of screenwriting, and part of its eloquence. The length of a screenplay requires the writer to have a clear vision of the heart of the story and the essential ingredients of the journey the writer is creating. Mark Twain once wrote, "Sorry this letter is so long, I didn't have time to write a short one." The screenplay is the short one. It condenses the essence of a major life transformation down to an hour and a half, in an entertaining way. This length restriction naturally causes the archetypal beats to be strong in a movie. It gives movies their powerful impact.

Structure can be defined in various ways. According to Viki King, author of *How to Write a Movie in 21 Days*, structure is "a chronology of your character's growth" (King, 42). Robert McKee sees structure as "a selection of events from a life story that are composed into a strategic sequence to arouse specific emotions and a specific view of life" (McKee, 33).

I define archetypal structure as "the bones upon which a story hangs." It is a set of patterns and images within the human collective unconscious, which are the roadmaps for the universal transformations of life. The archetypal structure of the Hero has been available for decades through the analysis of Joseph Campbell and Christopher Vogler. The *Virgin's Promise* introduces a theory for the progression of another archetypal structure. Every person inherits these archetypes and their patterns of behavior. How a person experiences them and brings them to life is what makes each life unique and interesting. The natural emergence of these archetypes in stories is what Blake Snyder describes as the thing studio executives are always looking for when they say "give me the same only different" (Snyder, 21).

The Three-Act Structure

In this theory, all stories are constructed of three parts: the beginning, the middle, and the end, otherwise known as Act I, Act II, and Act III. The pacing of the story is inherent to the three-act structure with each act being completed in a certain number of pages as shown in Table 6. Within each act there are several archetypal beats that must be accomplished. Notice the timing of key moments like the inciting incident and the moment of doubt differ for the Virgin and the Hero.

TABLE 6. Archetypal Beats Combined with Three-Act Structure

	VIRGIN	HERO
ACT I		
	1. Dependent World	1. Ordinary World
	2. Price of Conformity	2. Call to Adventure (inciting incident)
	3. Opportunity to Shine (inciting incident)	3. Refusal of the Call
	4. Dresses the Part	4. Meeting with the Guide
		5. Crossing the First Threshold

-------------------------------- page 30 --------------------------------

	VIRGIN	HERO
ACT II		
	5. The Secret World	6. Tests, Allies, Enemies
	6. No Longer Fits Her World	7. Preparations
	7. Caught Shining	
	8. Gives Up What Kept Her Stuck	8. Crisis (moment of doubt)
	9. Kingdom in Chaos	9. Reward

-------------------------------- page 90 --------------------------------

	VIRGIN	HERO
ACT III		
	10. Wanders in the Wilderness (moment of doubt)	10. The Road Back
	11. Chooses Her Light	11. Final Battle
	12. Re-ordering/Rescue	12. Return with the Elixir
	13. The Kingdom Is Brighter	

-------------------------------- page 120 --------------------------------

ACT I

In Act I, the protagonist is introduced to the audience with his/her fundamental strengths and weaknesses. We see the world in which s/he has been raised and come to understand the protagonist's compelling need for growth. This is the **Dependent World** of the Virgin, and the **Ordinary World** of the Hero.

This need for growth is expressed as a specific question, formed in the audience's mind, which the movie sets out to answer. For example, will the protagonist go against what others want for her and follow her own dream (as in Virgin stories)? Specifically, will Elle stop trying to land a husband and become her own kind of lawyer (*Legally Blond*)? Or, will the protagonist leave the village and save it from impending doom (as in Hero stories)? Specifically, will Axel Foley learn to work as a team player and avenge his friend's murder in *Beverly Hills Cop*? This central question must be embedded in the first act, subtly.

The inciting incident sets the story in motion and draws the main character into the story line (Field, 129). For the Virgin, it is the **Opportunity to Shine** and a joyful first taste of realizing her dream. It is the moment in *Strictly Ballroom* where Fran offers to dance non-Federation steps with Scott. The **Call to Adventure** is the inciting incident of the Hero's story. It is a disturbing moment where the Hero is called upon to leave his comfortable home and face death. It is the point in *Blood Diamond* where Danny meets Maddy and challenges him to take action against the diamond smuggling consortium.

The inciting incident in the Virgin story occurs somewhat later than in the Hero story. In the Virgin story two major beats are established prior to revealing the dream of the Princess. The audience is introduced to her normal life including the dependent nature of her domestic realm that keeps her locked into this world. She is also shown to be diminished by this environment (**Price of Conformity**) before we see the light flicker in her eyes at the **Opportunity to Shine**. The Hero story only has to show a normal life before the **Call to Adventure** then lays out the inciting incident and the question starts to form as to whether the Hero is up for the challenge.

Before entering Act II, the protagonist must have a clear goal and there must be difficulties in achieving it. The Virgin's dream or true nature is established along with its conflict with the kingdom's vision for her life. The joy of first expressing a measure of her true self, or the feeling of acknowledging her dream, creates a positive emotional peak and a momentary suspension of the hardship of her life at the end of Act I. In the case of the Hero, a problem is placed before him that he alone can tackle. By the end of Act I, despite initial reluctance, the Hero accepts the challenge, and faces fear of the unknown with a recognition that some things are worth dying for.

ACT II

Act II is the longest act of the story, and therefore most at risk of dragging. For the Virgin, the creation of the **Secret World** and the movement back and forth to the **Dependent World**, always fearful of discovery but joyful in the awakening of her dream, keep the action moving. Although she manages to appease her **Dependent World** she is growing uncomfortable with keeping her true self secret. Eventually, her secret is revealed and her kingdom goes into chaos. She leaves Act II realizing she has outgrown her **Dependent World** and facing the consequences of that new reality.

The Hero must come to fully recognize the problem at hand in Act II, gather allies and develop skills to eliminate the threat to the village in the next act. He also experiences a moment of doubt where he questions if he can survive facing death in the **Crisis**. His elation at facing death and still being alive encourages him just before the low point of mounting obstacles in **The Road Back** that takes the protagonist into Act III.

ACT III

In Act III, the Virgin must decide if she is going to go back to appeasing her **Dependent World** or follow her dream and deal with the consequences. She **Wanders in the Wilderness** during this moment of doubt, considering the cost of being herself and her ability to stand alone. The Virgin **Chooses Her**

Light and decides she will live according to her potential. The kingdom is then forced into a transformation to provide space for the Virgin to thrive or lose her. This may be a noble struggle to adjust its thinking out of love for the Virgin. Or it may be a backlash against the Virgin, which reveals an element of society that must be eliminated. These create a double climax of transformation: first the Virgin claims her true self, and then the kingdom struggles and grows to create a space where the Virgin can flourish and becomes a better place.

The Hero in Act III is taking the transformation that occurred when he faced death and testing it to the limits of his mortality. He squares off with the villain and asserts his will for the benefit of his village.

Act III also ties up all the loose ends, leaving the world in a position of stability. Either the kingdom has changed and found a new and improved equilibrium (Virgin stories) or the danger has been eliminated and the village is preserved or restored (Hero stories).

The emotional highs differ for Virgin and Hero stories. While both include moments of joy and fear, the Virgin quests to know joy and therefore the climax of her story is joyful. The Hero is overcoming fear and his story builds through mounting dangers until fear is conquered in the **Final Battle**.

These are the guidelines for structuring a screenplay; however, they may be varied or broken to create a desired effect. Archetypal structure is very robust. You can alter the order of the beats, skip a beat and have it implied, or repeat a beat for emphasis, and still create a screenplay that resonates with audiences.

An excellent example of beat flexibility is seen in the Hero story *The Bourne Identity*, where Jason has amnesia and has to build an **Ordinary World (1)** in the first half of the film, in the form of his relationship with Marie, while simultaneously exploring the foreign land of trained assassins and his old life (**Tests, Allies, Enemies** (6)). Jason's comfort zone (1) becomes time spent with Marie where he can rest as she talks. In the second half of the story, when Jason fully realizes who he was, he **Refuses the Call** (3) and tries to avoid the quest to rejoin his life, which calls him to correct the unchecked CIA project, Treadstone, that uses specially trained agents as "killing machines." These agents are now trying to eliminate Jason, endangering Marie and her friends, and must be stopped (5, 8). In this way, beat 3 is tucked between beats 6 and 8 with a very powerful result. Presenting the beats in this order recreates the experience of being a person with amnesia.

Archetypal structure is not intended to be a cookie cutter method for story writing. It is a highly flexible guide that accesses the power of the unconscious. Structure helps the writer make the selections that illuminate the heart of a story. It clarifies how and why the story works and promotes the removal of clutter.

The Beat Sheet

Archetypal structure is best applied early but can be applied at any stage of the writing process. It can be used to:

1. develop an outline for drafting a screenplay;
2. create a central question to focus the writing and re-writing;
3. develop character profiles with the power of archetypes;
4. write a brief summary or synopsis based on one or two sentences per beat, and
5. prepare for pitch sessions.

The first step in fleshing out the archetypal structure of a screenplay is to determine if it is a Virgin or Hero story. If the protagonist has a dream she wants to realize, be it winning a hockey cup, becoming an artist or asserting her views of governance, it is a Virgin story. If she wants to be accepted for her sexual, religious, fashion, or dance choices, and her family is dead set against it, it is a Virgin story. On the other hand, if the protagonist is called upon to protect, sustain, avenge, or restore others, and must travel to a foreign land and face near-certain death to do it, it is a Hero story.

It is not necessary for a character to be one archetype throughout the movie. A character may shift from one to another. Most often, there are moments of acting from the shadow side, for example when the Hero Refuses the Call, momentarily playing the Coward. A character may also progress from one light side archetype to another such as from the Virgin to the Mother/ Goddess when there is a love interest. The protagonist will usually embody a dominant archetype such as the Virgin or the Hero whose journey weaves a central thread through the movie.

Sometimes there is a choice of whether the story is best told from a Virgin or Hero perspective. *Erin Brockovich* is the story of a woman who sets out to stop a large corporation from poisoning people and wants the affected people compensated. This is a Hero story. However, it is based on a true story where the antagonist is a faceless corporation who does battle in boring scientific study-based arguments in court which doesn't play well on the screen. But the writer noticed it is also the story of Erin, a single, ex-beauty queen, uneducated mother of three who wants to help people in need. A girl with a dream. The antagonist now becomes everyone who fails to see Erin's potential or blocks her from realizing that dream, including the secretaries who won't help her and the lawyers who disrespect her. This is a more interesting movie.

A protagonist may follow the path of the Virgin from beginning to end or follow the journey of the Hero from beginning to end. Also, two archetypal structures create opportunities for several variations. The protagonist may be simultaneously a Virgin and a Hero, as in *Mulan*, where she is unsuited for the traditional roles of a daughter in China. Her talent lies in invention, strategy, and leadership. By fulfilling her talents, like a Virgin, Mulan also saves her father from certain death and her country from the Huns, as required by a Hero.

The protagonist may also progress from one archetype to another, undergoing two archetypal journeys in succession. In *Happy Feet*, Mumble is a penguin with a passion for dancing when all the other penguins are singers. As a Virgin he must be true to himself and dance. When his village is then threatened, Mumble undergoes the journey of a Hero and rescues the other penguins from humans. Alternatively, a simultaneous Virgin and Hero story can run through the movie in separate characters, either as dual protagonists or as a protagonist and a strong supporting character. Supporting characters can display only the parts of their archetypal journey that intersect with the protagonist's.

There are natural cross-over points between the Virgin and the Hero stories. During **Tests, Allies, Enemies** the Hero may first meet the Virgin in his foreign land (which is her **Dependent or Secret World**). The Virgin may become one of the Hero's allies. He may not be attracted to her at first because she is yet to present her true self. In this way, the Virgin's attractiveness is tightly linked to her authenticity. She may also become a representation of the feminine that inspires the Hero to be brave. In return, the Hero's attention provides the Virgin with encouragement to return to her **Secret World** and continue to grow. This is seen in *Ever After*, where the moments of seeing the Prince become her **Secret World**. The same situation occurs in *Maid in Manhattan* and *While You Were Sleeping*.

The Hero could also support the Virgin in the **Re-ordering**. The Hero's need to selflessly face danger to preserve something of value is compatible with the Virgin's need to be recognized as valuable in her authentic form and reconnected with her community. The Hero also satisfies the kingdom's need for **Re-ordering**, even if it puts up a fight. The Hero restores order in the kingdom after the chaos created by the Virgin's journey – a new, improved order that includes the Virgin fulfilling her dream. In *Working Girl*, when Jack lays his job on the line and tells Mr. Trask that he had better listen to Tess he is both behaving as a Hero and **Re-ordering** the Virgin's kingdom.

Appendix 1 provides a worksheet for describing each of the beats of a Virgin or Hero story with one or two sentences. The basic structure can be reworked by changing the order of the beats, repeating a beat for emphasis, or leaving a beat implied.

The beat sheet is useful in the redrafting process to highlight beats that are not included and consider whether adding them would strengthen the story. Also, sections of a screenplay that do not address any of the archetypal beats may be areas where the screenplay can be shortened. Even great dialogue that doesn't pull the story forward is clutter.

When creating an archetypal beat sheet, writing from memory is a good way to access the archetypal elements. As seen in oral cultures, the archetypal beats are often the ones most easily brought forward from memory. Moving through the beats, going back when an idea occurs, and brainstorming possible ideas where a beat is not represented, helps fill in the archetypal structure. One beat often shines light on another and revelations come.

The Central Question

As mentioned, the central question forms in the audience's mind in Act I and is answered in the climax of Act III. In psychological terms, the central question is a combination of the complex that is holding the protagonist back and the act of individuation that is drawing her forward.

Framing the heart of the story as a question puts the writer in the position of the audience. Subplots, jokes, and visual symbols can then be related to the central question to connect the audience to the screenplay on many levels. Writing a well-defined central question focuses the writing process and is best done right after drafting the beat sheet, before writing any dialogue.

CENTRAL QUESTION OF A VIRGIN STORY

The archetypal beat sheet can be used to draw out the central question of your screenplay. For example, in Virgin stories, combining the **Price of Conformity** with **Opportunity to Shine** creates a powerful statement of the essence of the story. The **Price of Conformity** is essentially what the Virgin gives up in **Gives Up What Kept Her Stuck**. Likewise, the **Opportunity to Shine** is the first step along the path towards bringing the dream of the Virgin to life, which is achieved in **Chooses Her Light**. Making strong connections between these four beats creates a well-focused screenplay.

The central question is most powerful when there is a strong incompatibility between **Gives Up What Kept Her Stuck** and **Chooses Her Light**. It must be impossible to realize her dream unless she changes the belief that is blocking her. The more incompatible the two sections, the more engaging the story.

A central question can be drafted by combining a description of the protagonist, followed by the complex with its behavior or belief that needs to stop, and a specific transformation that represents the Virgin coming into being. This creates a rhythmic statement that, as seen in oral traditions, helps to focus the thought.

For example, the central question for *The Sound of Music* would be, Will the apprentice nun, Maria, stop believing she needs the protection of the church walls and find a place for her zest for life? Maria grew up looking over the convent walls and wanting that safety. Her **Price of Conformity** is trying to control her desire to roam the hills and sing in order to earn a place in the convent where she feels safe. The **Opportunity to Shine** occurs when Maria is sent to take care of the Captain's eight children with whom she can roam and sing. Being a nun is in high contrast to, and incompatible with, marrying an Austrian captain with eight children. The conflict makes the story interesting.

More central questions are:

Will the Hispanic chambermaid, Marisa, stop conforming to class structure and become a manager? – *Maid in Manhattan*

Will orphaned Danielle stop being servile to her stepmother to earn parental love, and gain her rightful place in society? – *Ever After*

Will the coal miner's son, Billy, stop worrying about being assumed gay and become a ballet dancer? – *Billy Elliot*

Will ex-beauty queen Erin stop being dependent on unreliable men and realize her dream of making the world a better place (through crusading environmental claims)? – *Erin Brockovich*

Will the cowboy, Ennis, stop denying his sexuality and join society as a gay person? – *Brokeback Mountain*

Will rich and beautiful Elle stop believing she is a frivolous blond and learn to be her own kind of lawyer? – *Legally Blond*

Will the East Indian girl, Jas, stop being afraid to assert her wishes when they conflict with her parents' traditional Indian values, and play organized soccer? – *Bend It Like Beckham*

In the above examples the description of the protagonist is based on an external or socially imposed feature of the Virgin. Being rich, Hispanic, or a cowboy comes with societal assumptions but has no relation to her dream. The true nature of the Virgin is dormant and at odds with the role she is playing for society.

Another variation in the central question is when the potential for the Virgin is visible in the protagonist description but needs to be redirected. The science geek Casey has a gift for science but she needs to use it to make herself a better skater rather than assert her mom's sense of place for women in a man's world. This type of central question would read:

Will the science geek, Casey, stop rejecting her femininity to please her mom and become a competitive figure skater? – *Ice Princess*

Will orphaned John stop protecting his heart with superficial relationships and open himself to a meaningful relationship? – *Wedding Crashers*

In some stories there are two central questions; one for the main plot and one for the subplot. This can create a story with more depth as long as the two plots are well focused and don't work against each other. The protagonist should have lots of conflict but the screenplay should not have structural incompatibility. It is useful to write a central question for each plot and subplot to maximize clarity.

Will the street worker, Vivian, stop believing the "bad stuff" her family says about her and find meaningful work? – *Pretty Woman*

Will the street worker, Vivian, stop giving her heart to men who don't respect her and be truly loved and valued by her Prince Charming? – *Pretty Woman*

Will royalties-dependent Will stop believing he has to be an island and find a meaningful relationship? – *About a Boy*

Will the son of a one-hit-wonder stop fearing public embarrassment and pursue a career in music? – *About a Boy*

CENTRAL QUESTION FOR A HERO STORY

For Hero stories, the central question lies in combining the **Refusal of the Call** with the **Call the Adventure**. Again, the answer to this question is found in the **Crisis**, which resolves the complex, and the **Final Battle** where the Hero's transformation is complete. Here are a few examples:

Will renegade cop Axel Foley learn to work as a team member and successfully avenge the death of his childhood friend? – *Beverly Hills Cop*

Will diamond smuggler Danny recognize he is a part of Africa and reveal the information that will stop diamond buyers from fueling the violence? – *Blood Diamond*

Will ex-gunslinger William bring his skills as a man in balance with his love for his deceased wife, and avenge the wrong done to the whores? – *Unforgiven*

Will Mitch remember his love of the law and stop the firm's shady practices? – *The Firm*

Will cigarette scientist Jeff Wiegand overcome his fear of power and expose the health risks being hidden by profit-driven cigarette companies? – *The Insider*

Connections

Once the central question is well defined, the beat sheet can be revised to embed this clear understanding of the drive throughout the story. There are many connections that can be made between the beats that support the central question.

The belief the Virgin holds that needs to change, found in **Gives Up What Kept Her Stuck,** is foreshadowed in the **Price of Conformity.** It is generally rooted in something the Virgin feels she must believe or do to secure love or safety. In *Strictly Ballroom,* Scott wants to dance his own steps. His dance club has groomed him to win the next Federation competition and convinces him he must stick to traditional steps. His **Price of Conformity** is suppressing his personal dance expression. In **Gives Up What Kept Her Stuck** Scott learns from Fran's' family and his dad that it is the dancing that matters, not his ego or the opinion of the judges. The strong link between these two beats strengthens the story.

The more incompatible the **Dependent World** and **Chooses Her Light** are, the more gripping the story will be. Being a good, traditional Indian girl and a soccer star are incompatible. Being a cowboy and openly gay is not a recipe for survival. These are the set ups for conflict that get the story rolling.

In the overall picture of the Virgin's transformation, **Dresses the Part** is the first in a progression of related steps that are instrumental in bringing her true nature or dream to life. During **Dresses the Part** the Virgin converts the dream into something tangible, moving it from the ethereal to a private world. She does this by taking up the **Opportunity to Shine**, which is in a small setting in the presence of trusted friends or strangers. This becomes the **Secret World:** a cocoon in which the Virgin finds the space to develop. Finally, during **Chooses Her Light,** the Virgin's dream is introduced to the entire kingdom as the Virgin presents her true self in a larger setting. **Opportunity to Shine, Dresses the Part, Secret World** and **Chooses Her Light** all need to be related to the same dream and show a progression from a small world to a larger world.

The **Re-ordering** is related to the **Dependent World** in a satisfying pay-off structure. The dangers that caused the Virgin to conform to her **Dependent World** rise up against her when she **Chooses Her Light,** which inspires the **Re-ordering (Rescue).** The Virgin made herself small in the beginning to hold danger at bay. She grows to her full potential, which is a rebellion against her kingdom, and the feared danger rears its ugly head. Banishment from her community can put the Virgin in spiritual or even physical danger. The cost of the Virgin shining her light supports all her previous efforts to remain concealed.

Gives Up What Kept Her Stuck, Wanders in the Wilderness and **Chooses Her Light** form the three steps towards psychological transformation of the Princess. Noted sociologist Victor Turner recognized this pattern to human transformation which begins with separation from a past belief, followed by a liminal stage where one dwells between the two worlds and finally a stage of transformation where the person is healed (Turner, 94). The Virgin must separate from a belief she holds that is not serving her well in **Gives Up What Kept Her Stuck**. This leads to **Wandering in the Wilderness** which is a period of transition where she is not sure where she belongs, weighs the cost of going back and making everyone else happy or fulfilling her dream, until she **Chooses Her Light** and claims a new place for herself.

The kingdom also goes through the three phases of transformation to make room for the Virgin. First the **Kingdom goes into Chaos** where it disconnects from its old values. It then goes through a period of uncertainty and a battle of wills, the **Re-ordering**. This may include a backlash towards the Virgin, in which case there is a **Rescue**. Finally, in **The Kingdom Is Brighter** stage decisions are made to embrace the Virgin and her dream and the kingdom becomes a better place to live.

Numerous connections to the central question are evident in good movies. The central question in *Billy Elliot* is, will the coal miner's son, Billy, stop worrying about being assumed gay and become a ballet dancer? It is a story of a boy becoming a ballet dancer where attitudes regarding masculinity and femininity are the obstacle to dancing. Billy wants to dance in the distinctly feminine world of ballet while his **Dependent World** is completely masculine. With this understanding, you can see the story is loaded with representations of masculinity and femininity and their relative value in life. Billy's mother has died, which emphasizes the lack of feminine values in his world. Billy is left to care for his grandmother, who is barely hanging onto reality and is treated like a burden. In essence, Billy is left trying to keep the last bit of feminine presence alive in his home. This is a strong metaphor for what he is trying to do through his dancing.

This dwindling loss of femininity and the corrosive effect on his father is graphically depicted at Christmas where Billy's mother's piano has to be burned for heat. The feminine value of joy and music is sacrificed for the masculine value of providing shelter and safety. Physicality is favored over verbal communication when the brothers are together, in the boxing lessons, or in the actions of the striking miners. Fear, loyalty, and the need to provide are played against joy, beauty, and sensuality throughout the movie.

In the conclusion, Billy's dad and brother go to the ballet. They leave their small town and experience expansive architecture, music, and dance. All these features are symbolic of Billy's impact. He has brought a measure of feminine values into their lives and the men are happier and full of wonder because of it.

In *Beverly Hills Cop*, the central question is, will Axel Foley learn to work as a team member and avenge his friend's death? The opening scene with the cigarette-smuggling bust that goes bad and wreaks destruction all over town symbolizes the problem Axel has with being a team player. If he had followed procedure, his own people would not have busted him in the middle of a sting operation.

Axel's lack of connection to his team is emphasized by his incongruent background. Most of the cops are Irish looking and probably the sons of cops. Axel is black and grew up in a poor neighborhood on a path to becoming a criminal along with his friends. This establishes Axel as an outsider. However, Axel's boss is also black, suggesting that systemic discrimination against blacks is not the issue. This is Axel's personal inability to rationalize the neighborhood he came from with the job he has chosen. When his old friend shows up suggesting he help him in criminal activity, Axel is pulled between two worlds as his allegiance is tested. Is he going to follow the code of law and turn his back on the friend who kept him from going to jail or is he going to help his friend and risk his career? And will Axel ignore his boss's direct order and go to Los Angeles to avenge his friend's murder or will he let police procedure take its course?

All of these scenes address the issue of belonging to a team and express the character of Axel.

Romantic and humorous scenes are much more powerful when they are related to the archetypal theme. An example is the humorous moments in *Beverly Hills Cop*, which are directly related to the question, "Will Axel learn to work as a team member?" When Axel places a banana in the tailpipe of the Los Angeles cops' car, he is making fools of people with whom he is supposed to be working. When Axel spins a lie to get the Los Angeles cops out of trouble with their superior officer and the Los Angeles cops confess, it is funny as Axel tries to understand their curious behavior. These moments are funnier and contribute to the pace of the story because they relate to the heart of the movie.

Connections to the central question give a movie a satisfying feeling of depth. Jokes, visual images and dialogue can be infused with symbolic representations of the central question and its relevance to the archetypal growth of the protagonist.

Character Profiles and Symbolism

Once the central question is established, it can be used to create compelling characters through symbolism. Symbols are the language of archetypes. The goal is to find character traits and actions that express the central question and the archetypal essence of the story. The essential nature of each archetype as described in Chapter One, Archetypal Theory, needs to be symbolically represented in the characters of a screenplay. Appendix 3 provides a worksheet for developing character profiles.

A tool for illuminating the archetypal essence of each character is to juxtapose opposites: feminine to masculine, shadow to light. Placing the Virgin and the Hero together strengthens the image of each. Placing the Virgin with the Whore or the Hero with the Coward also generates symbolic energy. Superheroes are often portrayed with this technique. The Hero rarely shows fear but the Coward beside him, usually a sidekick, keeps the Hero's bravery from becoming monotonous. Alternatively, the shadow side archetype can emerge in the protagonist temporarily, making later actions more poignant. For example, Vivian opens *Pretty Woman* as the Whore, and Luke Skywalker plays the Coward when he refuses the call to adventure in the opening of *Star Wars*.

The following section is not an exhaustive look at the symbolic representations of each archetype as they can be symbolized in an infinite number of ways. Furthermore, repeated use of the same representations results in stereotypes and the loss of archetypal power. This section provides examples of how the essential natures of the twelve core archetypes have been effectively symbolized in the past. These are offered as an avenue for connecting with their place in the collective unconscious where new symbolic representations of the archetypes can be stimulated. The unique ways a writer finds to achieve this symbolism makes storytelling fresh and engaging. Finding the symbol always begins with knowing the essential nature of the archetype.

Symbols of the Virgin

This beginning stage of the feminine journey to claim one's interior world or personal authority is often visually represented by female youth. Virginity is used to symbolize pristine, unspoiled nature as in a virgin forest and the beauty of simply being. It also speaks to the untapped potential of life.

The Virgin represents innocence and naivety and is therefore a susceptible target in power games. She is treated as a valued commodity because of her role in the continuation of cultural values and patriarchy. This is symbolized by praise for her purity and sexual inexperience, which hold the promise of controlling bloodlines. The Virgin's beauty is traded for its potential to improve family status and security through marriage, servitude or image. The gowns and jewels the Virgin wears represent the status of her family. The Virgin may dress as a boy to symbolize the need to shed the societal expectations placed on girls.

The dependent nature of the Virgin can be portrayed by setting the story in a time when laws prohibited women from owning property or having jobs or choosing whether to marry. Cultural traditions also demonstrate the Virgin in her dependent role. Wedding ceremonies, funeral gatherings, ethnic meals and traditional dress all richly symbolize the powerful influences of cultural and religious traditions on the Virgin as her compliance is required for their transmission to future generations.

Remaining in the domestic realm of her childhood graphically illustrates that the Virgin has not separated from the influences of the people she grew up with. She is surrounded by people who seek to instill values in her, plan her future, control her social interactions including sexual orientation, or control the use of her time. She is dependent on them for safety, nurturance and a sense of self. Being young, or a young orphan, emphasizes the legitimacy of the Virgin's need to exist within the boundaries people establish for her (*Little Miss Sunshine, Angels in the Outfield, Billy Elliot*).

The Virgin's suppressed true self is introduced through an unproven dream, a unique way of viewing the world, or a dormant talent. The suppressed dream of the Virgin may be revealed through images on her bedroom wall or activities she engages in secretly. Longingly observing the actions of someone else also conveys the dreams of the Virgin. Joining rallies and protests against impossible odds, or dreaming of being a journalist, symbolize her need to be heard and represented in the world. Conversely, a lousy boyfriend is a metaphor for living out of step with her authentic self, as seen in *The Wedding Singer, Working Girl* and *Legally Blond*.

The Virgin has an inkling in her heart of her potential, despite the complete lack of tangible proof or support. A small voice, awkwardness, and insecurity portray the lack of confidence that comes with being an unproven entity. Presenting an image of being helpless, dutiful, acting dumb, or making herself small shows the Virgin's reluctance to bring forward her true self and provides a strong contrast to the end of her journey when she knows her feminine power.

A major challenge for the Virgin story is representing the development of a relationship with one's self on screen. Beauty is often used to symbolize a reflection of soul and establish her inner world as valuable and worth bringing to life. The beauty of the Virgin is commonly described with metaphors of light: radiant, luminous, brilliant, shining, beaming, or glowing. "He flashed a smile"; "her skin was lustrous." Schenk believes the notion of light is essential to the world of beauty (Schenk, 60). Light represents perception, knowing, and being. It is related to being visible. Light serves the sensual function of revealing and in the case of beauty revealing the soul. Seemingly mundane activities like choosing a special outfit, painting her nails, and putting on make-up to enhance her beauty all symbolize the desire to express and celebrate her unique self. Transforming from an ugly duckling to a beautiful swan shows the development of a relationship with herself.

Closeness to nature is another metaphor for connecting with herself. Walking in the woods or the advice of an earthy best friend can be the voice of self needing to be heard. A best friend can represent the Virgin's internal dialogue between the expectations of others and her desire for herself. Talking to an animal or the image of a deceased loved one also symbolizes the Virgin's effort to make a connection with her soul.

Alternatively, the Virgin can be shown to be out of touch with herself by appearing dormant. She may actually go to sleep, become seriously ill, depressed, or go into a coma to demonstrate that a part of her must be awakened. The name Sleeping Beauty is a great word image for the Virgin. It puts together the radiance of her soul with her inactivity, which feels like a loss.

The Princess needs to bring a piece of her soul into being. The art of being can be represented by any creative act where the inspiration comes from within such as dancing, singing or painting. It can also be a spiritual act of believing in a greater power such as following a calling or wish fulfillment. The act of sexual awakening is another powerful metaphor for discovering and claiming a part of herself.

Table 7. The Virgin as a Symbol

	stage	relationship	essence	a.k.a.
Virgin	beginning	to self, to emotional/ internal needs	dependent, out of step, radical, seeking self-fulfillment, joy, dream fulfillment, creative, spiritual, sexual awakening	Princess, Maiden, Misfit, Prince, Artist, Rebel, Magical Child

Symbols of the Whore

The Whore has lost authority over her life and is an unvalued and scorned commodity in society. She provides no evidence that she has a dream for herself or the right to express a personal opinion. She has lost touch with her soul, which is often represented by loss of control over her sexuality. People control where she lives or how she spends her time.

The distinction between the Whore and the Virgin is that the Virgin is asleep to her potential, which is preserved but dormant. The Whore knows she is selling or being robbed of her soul but feels powerless to reclaim it. The ugliness of life graphically surrounds her because the Whore is awake to her situation. The internal nature of her journey is shown by her spiral downward into shame, depression, isolation, and insanity.

Negative societal judgment of the Whore is shown by placing the Whore in a world without the protection of a community. The Whore is seen under the control of a criminal or patriarchal environment with low respect for feminine values. She is devalued by her kingdom's negative judgment and victimized.

Classically, the Whore is represented as a sex worker, often young and female with revealing clothes, excessive makeup, spike heels, and wigs. She dresses to excite others' fantasies rather than to fulfill her dream. Her face (true potential) is hidden behind a mask of make-up or a pasted smile.

Another representation of the Whore can be the Stepford-type wife whose face is unreadable and who spends her days meeting the needs of her family at the expense of knowing herself (this is very different from the giving of the Mother/Goddess that comes from a place of knowing one's power). She dresses to look respectable and please her husband and works endlessly without recognition or reward (*The Banger Sisters*).

The masculine Whore can be represented by the chump husband who complies with a wife who emotionally manipulates and abuses him. The Whore is also the clown who smiles and gives the crowd what it wants while his heart is sad.

TABLE 8. The Whore as a Symbol

	stage	relationship	essence	a.k.a.
Whore	beginning	to self, to emotional/ internal needs	victimized, loss of soul, insane, depressed, suicidal	Prostitute, Victim, Slave, Sad Clown, Damsel

SYMBOLS OF THE MOTHER/GODDESS

The Mother/Goddess archetype is on a middle stage journey to enter into a relationship with another that brings joy and emotional connection. She is often portrayed as an adult woman who knows her spiritual, sensual, and creative powers and generously uses them to nurture and inspire others. Her need is to join with the masculine in a relationship that feeds and regenerates her powers. She needs to find a home that replenishes her by developing the art of receiving.

The Mother/Goddess is represented as self-confident with a soft beauty that reveals her passions and origins. Round, smooth, and curvaceous shapes bring forward the Mother/Goddess's feminine sensuality, often mirrored in architecture, furniture, images of nature, or body forms. The Mother/Goddess is also symbolized by water, images of nourishment such as sumptuous meals, and gardens lush with flowers.

The Mother/Goddess may be a mother or a father engaged in creative play and expressions of unconditional love with children. She creates a home that welcomes, inspires, and nourishes its inhabitants. She makes people's senses come alive with color, sound, smell, and seasonal celebrations. Her child-birthing capacity speaks to her Goddess-like powers. The Mother/Goddess produces life and, through the continuation of inherited qualities, immortality.

The way the Mother/Goddess spends money is a good expression of her values. She spends money to celebrate life, to empower other people to follow their dreams, and to experience creativity, joy, spirituality, and beauty.

The challenge of the Mother/Goddess is to form a relationship with the masculine despite their polar opposite drives. She inspires change and chaos as people around her allow themselves to explore passion and joy. They express feelings, fail to obey orders, miss work. This often flies in the face of masculine order, judgment, and control. This clash of values is symbolized by the Mother Goddess facing court proceedings, impending deadlines, financial hardships, and social conspiracies to isolate her. The clash of the masculine and the feminine depletes the Mother/Goddess. The rejuvenation of these powers may come from a love interest, a supportive community or a discovery of a place of rejuvenation in a creative activity or spiritual path.

TABLE 9. The Mother/Goddess as a Symbol

	stage	relationship	essence	a.k.a.
Mother/Goddess	middle	to another, receives another human being into her heart, internal, emotional	nurturing, joyful inspiring, sensual awakening, creates love, ecstasy	Healer, Storyteller, Priestess, Visionary, Alchemist, Father, God, Priest, Samaritan

SYMBOLS OF THE FEMME FATALE

The Femme Fatale is aware of her power over the emotions and drives of others and uses it for her maximum personal benefit. She rejuvenates herself by invoking jealousy, guilt, lust, and greed to manipulate people but her behavior repels meaningful or lasting relationships. The Femme Fatale takes rather than receives.

The Femme Fatale's misuse of power is sometimes symbolized by the business woman in a mini-skirted power suit designed to detach men from their common sense and create her advantage. She is the lawyer who twists the law and pushes buttons to win a case rather than have justice prevail. She is the mother who twists her children's emotions until they are incapable of independent action. She may also appear helpless and admiring as she twists men to her bidding. Sometimes she's gorgeous but deadly, like a poisonous flower. Images of bright red lips, or shiny black body-skimming clothes evoke this aspect of her. As the lead female role in *The Matrix*, Trinity is interesting in that she has the visual appearance of a Femme Fatale but uses it to scare men away because she is afraid of her Mother/Goddess destiny. Her image is powerful because she juxtaposes the light and shadow sides of the same archetypal stage, namely the middle feminine journey.

The Femme Fatale arouses desires and vulnerabilities, which she uses to control others. The masculine reaction to the Femme Fatale is to feel emasculated rather than reborn through the relationship. The partner usually ends up crippled, impotent, jobless, viewed as weak, deflated or dead to represent this aspect of her.

The masculine version of the Femme Fatale is the Vampire, which aptly symbolizes the hopelessness of a relationship with this archetype. Seduced into the ecstasy of union, the partner has the blood sucked out of her until she's dead.

TABLE 10. The Femme Fatale as a Symbol

	stage	relationship	essence	a.k.a.
Femme Fatale	middle	to another, inspires hatred, mistrust, fear and stagnation, emasculates others	emotional manipulation, self focus, vengeful, moody, a taker	Bitch/Manipulator, Wicked Stepmother, Guilt-tripping Mother, Sleazy Lawyer, Gossip, Vampire

SYMBOLS OF THE CRONE

The Crone's quest is to release her power and join the cosmos. The Crone's powers of intuition and connection to nature have evolved to a magical level and she seeks to use them to facilitate people's transformations. She can do this with a helping hand, as the Fairy Godmother does, or through the chaos brought on by the Trickster that forces change.

The Crone character is often depicted as an independent woman with an ability to bring people to a crisis point of change through their love for her, or a quirky knack for saying things and showing up in places that causes pivotal life events. In some stories she has the ability to cast spells and invoke the weather. She may communicate with animals and provide them with advice or understanding.

Knowing what is best for other people symbolizes the Crone's union with the cosmos. Most often she is represented as an elderly woman. No longer occupied with child-rearing or being a mate, the Crone is a wanderer, a part of the bigger world, seeing the bigger picture. She is the old woman who casts a spell on the arrogant prince to make him a beast until he truly loves and earns love in return.

The Crone can also be young and take on the form of the Trickster. She is the best friend who messes things up or embarrasses others until the protagonist stumbles into the place where s/he is meant to be. The Jester, or the Fool, who makes the king laugh at her audacity to speak the truth, also embodies this archetype.

TABLE 11. The Crone as a Symbol

	stage	relationship	essence	a.k.a.
Crone	end	to the cosmos	to cause growth in others and join the cosmos	Guide, Fool, Exorcist, Jester, Trickster, Shapeshifter, Mystic

SYMBOLS OF THE HAG

According to Marion Woodman, "arriving at middle age is agony for those who cannot accept the mature beauty of autumn" (Woodman, 16). The Hag embodies resistance to joining the cosmos. This is often represented by an obsession with anti-aging or a focus on the past as a heyday or a preoccupation with the miseries of life and what could have been.

The effort to remain young may result in a grotesque or incongruent image. The wrinkled woman loaded down with make-up, wearing the plunging neckline of fashions designed for twenty-year-old breasts fits this image. Her breasts are a metaphor for the change in her role and the passage of time.

The Hag may use her magical powers to create the illusion she is young. These actions are a metaphor for her failure to embrace the end stage of life and form a relationship with something greater than herself. Instead she becomes an impediment to other people as they strive to move forward on their archetypal pathways. She may become competition for the Mother/Goddess and join with the Lover/King in a hopeless union. If she joins with the Hero, she confounds his efforts to stand on his own by hooking him into a Mother Complex. Her actions may be infused with a coldness and a harsh edge from life experience that cannot be concealed by the illusion.

Another representation of the Hag's resistance to joining the cosmos is to be backward-looking. Filled with regret and nostalgia, bemoaning better days, she strives to drag others down with her rather than embracing the spiritual aspect of moving forward towards death. This can be symbolized by a clothing style and hair from a past era, and by lines of disapproval and disappointment marking her face. Gross self-neglect can symbolize the complete lack of attachment to the beauty in her soul and her journey.

In male form, this archetype is the Lecher who lures young women with diamonds to entice them to satisfy his lust when the Virgin should be finding her own power. The Lecher has wrinkled and veined, greedy hands and focuses on satisfying his physical needs like an addict, rather than looking for greater meaning. A womanizer or shadow Don Juan seeks sexual conquest to deny his aging rather than a meaningful union with the feminine.

TABLE 12. **The Hag as a Symbol**

	stage	relationship	essence	a.k.a.
Hag	end	to cosmos	to cause stagnation in others and deny the existence of the cosmos	Witch, Thief, Saboteur, Cougar, Lecher, Don Juan

SYMBOLS OF THE HERO

The Hero must learn he can exist outside the nurturing environment of his mother and selflessly perform brave acts to secure his village. In the beginning, the Hero's physical needs for clothing, food, and shelter are met by the village. The Hero classically wears a regional style of clothing, emphasizing his connection to the village and his mother, lack of worldliness, and lack of independence. These clothes will also mark him as a stranger when he arrives at the foreign land.

Youth is often used to represent this beginning stage of archetypal growth with physical qualities such as slightly long hair and a smooth boyish face, be it male or female. Heroes are often male to exemplify the masculine nature of their journey. His quest to know he can survive in a bigger world is shown by the desire to develop skill, bravery and ruggedness. However, it is the nature of the quest as opposed to the gender of the person that defines the Hero.

The Hero isn't always a youthful character. He can also represent the beginning of a journey through his awkwardness, timidity or insecurity. The Hero is often undereducated and untraveled to depict his inexperience.

The Hero has a strong physical presence; he is built for action and facing adversity. Restlessness symbolizes his need for action. A sharp brain also demonstrates the Hero's readiness for action in a world of wits and intellectual maneuvering such as the courtroom or the political arena. His goodness may be represented by wearing white or light-colored clothing, riding a white horse on his journey to do good deeds, or showing kindness to his elders. Valuing his mother or the traditions and people of his village also demonstrate his goodness.

The Hero is often fascinated by weapons, protective equipment, and outdoor skills, showing his desire to expand the boundaries of his mortality and selflessly protect others. Jobs such as a fireman, an outdoor adventurer, a cowboy, a junior executive or a revolutionary soldier capture the Hero's nature as a loner and risk taker in service to others.

TABLE 13. The Hero as a Symbol

	stage	relationship	essence	a.k.a.
Hero	beginning	to self	bravery, skill, ruggedness, strength	Adventurer, Son, Heroine

SYMBOLS OF THE COWARD

The Coward is the shadow side of the Hero and therefore embodies fearfulness and a determination to secure personal comfort or safety.

The Coward may be physically represented by a weak and sickly nature, a small, soft, or pudgy physique covered by fussy, high-maintenance clothing. He may hide behind long, face-covering hair or have a high perceived need for the comforts of life. He complains about the food and longs for his own bed.

Closely attached to a protector, he is unwilling to leave his mother-figure, no matter what danger everyone else faces. He is a weasel who pushes others before him to face danger. He may stay close to home, or he may spin stories to avoid being called upon, duck out when danger is imminent. He is the able-bodied man trying to blend in with women, children, the elderly and the sick. Sometimes he lies, fakes injuries, betrays others, or makes up stories to avoid facing death.

In short, the Coward uses his resources to avoid putting himself in harm's way or having to provide for himself. Bullies, weaklings, and spoiled rich kids have been used as Coward symbols.

TABLE 14. The Coward as a Symbol

	stage	relationship	essence	a.k.a.
Coward	beginning	to self	fearful, hiding, self-preservation	Bully, Eternal Child

SYMBOLS OF THE LOVER/KING

The Lover/King is an image of an adult with benevolent power whose goal is to be of service to his community by providing the necessities of life including order, justice, and peace. The growth challenge of the Lover/King is to surrender to love in order to create a union with the feminine. He offers his heart and his services and allows the Mother/Goddess to become the source of meaning in his life.

Physically, the Lover/King is represented with strong lines, a larger physical presence than the Hero, and in the prime of life. He may have a strong jaw line, a mustache, short beard or manly five o'clock shadow, while his eyes and smile reveal his benevolence. His strength is apparent in his integrity or his influence over other people, largely obtained through respect. He is the boss, the head of the family, the corporate leader or judge. Through his leadership qualities he brings the force of law, tradition, and social order to the community.

Symbols of power that surround the Lover/King archetype commonly include judge's robes, an office with a view, a briefcase, a tasteful and well-organized apartment, or a powerful car. Alternatively, he may own a clunker car because he doesn't need to compensate for a weak ego by driving a Porsche. The Lover/King uses money to provide for and protect others, show intelligence which instills confidence, and amass power for good governance.

The Lover/King is also a symbol of virility and blessings. He is a provider, with strong life energy and charisma. He inspires excitement in women and is lusty in return, but with control. Always respectful to women, the Lover/King would put himself in harm's way for a woman, asking nothing for himself in return. He offers rather than exchanges his time and resources in relationships with other people.

TABLE 15. The Lover/King as a Symbol

	stage	Relationship	essence	a.k.a.
Lover/King	middle	to another, external, extends service to another	usefulness, chivalry, justice, order, safety, providing	Warrior, Mediator, Companion, Judge, Angel, Advocate

SYMBOLS OF THE TYRANT

The Tyrant is a middle stage masculine archetype who enters into relationships to amass power through intimidation and transactional giving. Physically he could be presented with icy-cold blue eyes, thin lips and a muscular machine-like physique. He classically wears dark colors, chunky jewelry to show his wealth, smokes (perhaps big stinky cigars to show his lack of concern for the comfort of others), drinks, and carries a gun. He has attachments to technical gadgets such as a cell phone, security gates, cameras, weaponry, and machinery like fast cars and helicopters.

The Tyrant leads through fear and asserts his power by inflicting pain. Participation in criminal activity, loan sharking, gambling, drug dealing and prostitution represent this aspect. He indulges in luxury for himself while others go in need or fawn around him for favor. He has many lackeys that do his dirty work for him.

The Tyrant is sexually oppressive, demanding that his needs be served. His sexual partners often remain generic and nameless, rotating over the course of a movie to demonstrate his lack of attachment. The Tyrant hates new life. He will go as far as to make war on his sons and daughters, and ruthlessly kill creativity (Moore, 64).

Structures of power like hierarchy and patriarchy are great metaphors for the Tyrant's competitive view of human relations, with himself at the top. He is often involved in dynasties, monarchies, social structures, and corporate ladders.

The female form of the Tyrant would be the Wicked Stepmother or the Evil Queen. Schenk suggests ugliness is best shown when a person's face does not match their soul (Schenk, 39). This is the case with great villains such as the Queen-stepmother in *Snow White* and Cruella de Ville in *101 Dalmatians*. They have all the cultural trappings of beauty but appear terrifyingly evil and ugly because their souls are not in sync with their appearance.

The Tyrant's relationships are based on reciprocity. He always asks the question, "What's in it for me?" He must never appear lower than the other guy, never be taken advantage of, and never give more than he gets. That's just not good business, in the Tyrant's mind. Jobs like head of a Mafia organization or a dictator portray this aspect of the Tyrant.

TABLE 16. The Tyrant as a Symbol

	stage	relationship	essence	a.k.a.
Tyrant	middle	to another, induces crime, usury, and terror	dominance, reciprocity, control, transactional	Destroyer, Dictator, Evil Queen, Wicked Stepmother

SYMBOLS OF THE MENTOR

The Mentor is often an elder to symbolize an end stage archetype. He is often male to represent the masculine drive to transfer money, knowledge, wisdom, and property to the next generation. Long gray hair and beard, as well as a wrinkled face, are effective ways to show the passage of time leading to his accumulation of assets. His hands appear giving and gnarly like trees.

The Mentor may carry a staff, an umbrella, or even a cane, which gives him a regal air, or indicates his place as the aging keeper of knowledge. He is well mannered and non-reactive when in relation to others, having an element of peaceful control and an understanding of the bigger picture. Slow moving and purposeful, he often wears clothing of a Merlin or Asian mystic style. He seeks out people rather than waiting for them to come to him, symbolizing his maturity and understanding of the time to transfer power.

Teaching the use of a weapon is a metaphor for the transference of power and the wisdom to use it well. The Mentor is looking to leave a lasting positive effect on Earth, which is represented by philanthropy work, building hospitals and schools, or placing benevolent leaders in positions of power.

TABLE 17. The Mentor as a Symbol

	stage	relationship	Essence	a.k.a.
Mentor	end	to cosmos, external	to pass wisdom and material accumulation on to others and leave a lasting positive effect	Merlin, Wise Woman, Wise Man, Philanthropist

SYMBOLS OF THE MISER

The Miser pays no attention to the spiritual opportunities of aging and instead clings tightly to the material things in life. He is stingy with his money, his time, and his connections, not even spending it on himself in some extremes. He invests his energy in storing, counting, protecting and hiding his assets. An image of an old man hunched over a box of gems wearing layers of tattered clothes to fight back the cold captures this archetype.

He hangs onto his material possessions so tightly he leaves other people neglected and impoverished. He becomes his own worst enemy, so suspicious that everyone is stealing his stuff that he is cut off from connection with people in the world and is miserable. The Miser will live in isolation to prevent anyone from stealing his ring. Images of his isolation include a lone person living in a big house that no one ever visits. If he showed up at a community gathering, people would stare.

TABLE 18. The Miser as a Symbol

	stage	relationship	essence	a.k.a.
Miser	end	to cosmos, neglects others leaving them to starvation, ignorance and instability	hoards, deprives others, neglects	Hermit, Spinster

The chart of the twelve core archetypes in Appendix 3 can be used to consider the symbolic representations of characters during the writing process. It can help focus their archetypal nature by comparison with the masculine, feminine, shadow and light side counterparts.

Conclusion

*I*n the collective unconscious of humans, there are archetypal journeys waiting to guide us through the universal transformations of life. This book is intended to activate those archetypes and bring them to writers' fingertips for the creation of engaging stories. *The Virgin's Promise* includes several ways to evoke the archetypes, including descriptions of their essential nature, proposed beats for the Virgin and Hero journeys, recognition of the beats in other movies, notes on the importance of symbols as the language of the unconscious, the use of memory to identify the archetypal story and the juxtaposition of opposites to give full effect to the archetypes. The goal is to access the feeling of resonance that accompanies a connection with the collective unconscious. As I did on my first day of film school, each writer has the ability to question and rearrange the notion of archetypes until s/he gets a feeling of resonance. It is that feeling that guides the writer into the world of archetypes.

Joseph Campbell excited a continent of storytellers and receivers when he put forward his theory of the Hero's Journey. For years writers have been asking for a similar roadmap for the unique journey of the feminine story. *The Virgin's Promise* is presented here as a structure for writing those feminine stories of bringing one's dream or true nature to life, which generally happens through creative, spiritual or sexual awakening.

Although Virgin stories have always existed, we now have a theory for their thirteen essential beats, making the structure more accessible. Together the Virgin and the Hero describe the two sides of learning to stand as an individual: the internal and emotional separation achieved by the Virgin, and the external and physical separation of the Hero. They also represent the two forms of coming into personal power: the power to be and the power to do.

The drive towards the personal growth of the Virgin and the Hero is tempered by complexes that hold a person back. According to Jungian theory, we have a mechanism of archetypes to pull us forward in the individuation process, to risk the unknown and grow, and a mechanism of complexes to guard against repeating the same mistakes. Individuation gives a sense of meaning in life and involves establishing a relationship to self, as the Virgin and Hero do, a relationship to others, as the Mother/Goddess and Lover/King do, and a relationship to the cosmos, as the Crone and the Mentor do. These themes exist in the collective unconscious and are excited when we recognize them in stories or along the writer's journey.

Movies are a natural medium for archetypal structure for two reasons. First, the language of archetypes is symbols. Images and metaphors conjure the archetypes in ways direct words cannot. Film, being a highly malleable and visual medium, can lace every scene with images that symbolize the archetypal meaning. For example, sexual union between the Virgin and the Hero symbolizes the Virgin's claim over her personal autonomy and drive towards joy as well as the Hero's elation at facing death and surviving. Symbols have the power to show, not tell, the journey of the protagonist.

Second, the restrictive length of a movie mimics the effect of memorization, clearing away the clutter, exposing the heart of the story. In oral traditions, stories were repeated from memory around the campfire, taking pieces of life and embellishing to give meaning, until they became the fairy tales and myths that form the roots of storytelling today. Memorization and distillation down to what can be told in ninety minutes continues to have the effect of bringing strong archetypal structure to a story.

This book adds an understanding of the Virgin's journey to reveal her promise, as shown in movies. The Virgin's promise speaks both to the societal expectation that she will fulfill a prescribed role, which is her burden, and her potential for being beautiful, talented, brilliant, and fabulous. In thirteen key beats, the Virgin exists in a **Dependent World** where she holds back her essential nature in order to conform to the dictates of others. She must know this poverty of personal expression, which is her **Price of Conformity**, in order to be driven towards fully being. One day she is given the **Opportunity to Shine** and she **Dresses the Part** she was born to fulfill. After this first experience of being true to herself, the Virgin establishes a **Secret World** where she grows in her dream, in a private act of rebellion. The Virgin moves back and forth between her **Secret World** and her **Dependent World**, always fearful of discovery, but joyful in her growth until she can no longer continue to make herself small to appease her kingdom. Her two worlds collide and she is **Caught Shining**. The **Kingdom Goes into Chaos**. The Virgin **Gives Up** the belief that was **Keeping Her Stuck** and consciously **Wanders in the Wilderness** between going back to the safety of pleasing others and the unknown of living by her own values. She **Chooses to Shine Her Light** and a backlash is vented on the Virgin as the kingdom is forced to **Re-order** itself. When a new equilibrium is reached, the **Kingdom Shines More Brightly** than before.

In this way the Virgin discovers the promise life holds for her as an individual. She interacts with other people such as the Hero to find inspiration, support, and reward for undergoing this transformation. A Virgin story is not about joining her life with another's.

Insight into the Virgin and the Hero archetypal journeys has several advantages for writers. The two journeys can be viewed relative to each other and offer new insights as they are recognized as the yin and yang of a whole. A clear understanding of the essential nature of the Virgin and the Hero as individuals facilitates stand-alone stories with rich metaphors and symbols. Knowing what it is not, helps define what it is. For example, the Virgin is driven towards joy and the Hero is driven away from fear. Together they represent two fundamental drives in human nature.

The Virgin and Hero archetypes center on the journey to know who they are as individuals. The Virgin is about self-fulfillment. She joyfully develops the art of being through awakening her creativity, spirituality and sexuality. She separates from her **Dependent World** and claims her personal authority in a form of second birth. In this way she works through the Father Complex, no longer allowing the values of patriarchy or culture to dictate her values or the use of her life. She also overcomes envy and its power to cause her to make herself small and deny her goodness in order to protect herself. The Virgin story is set in the domestic realm and brings chaos and change to the Kingdom, to its betterment. Coming of Age movies, wish-fulfillment movies, underdog sports movies, dreams-come-true themes and fairy tales are centered on the Virgin archetype in action.

The Hero is about self-sacrifice and overcoming fear through the development of bravery, ruggedness and skill. In this way he works through his Mother Complex and learns he can survive without her nurturing comforts. The story is set in a foreign land on the boundary between mortals and gods. The Hero battles evil to preserve his village and protect it from future threat of change. Action movies, horror films, murder mysteries, revenge plots, treasure hunts and myths are often derived from the Hero archetype in action.

The pacing of a Virgin story differs from a Hero Story. The inciting incident of a Virgin story occurs late in Act I after the Dependent World and the Price of Conformity are established. The moment of doubt is also later, occurring in Act III just before the double climax of the Virgin declaring her true self to her kingdom and the kingdom undergoing a restructuring to provide a place where she can flourish. The emotional highs in a Virgin film are moments of great joy while emotional peaks in a Hero story are moments of intense fear.

Virgin and Hero archetypes can be presented in a variety of combinations that add variety and bring a balance to masculine and feminine elements in storytelling. The juxtaposition of the feminine and the masculine has the benefit of making each more sharply defined on the screen. The same effect is created when the shadow side is placed beside the light side archetype; the Virgin beside the Whore or the Hero beside the Coward. These archetypal pairs can be represented in a single character or two characters working side by side. One defines the other and together they are intriguing.

Having two archetypal journeys gives writers new structural combinations for storytelling. A screenplay may be told from either the Virgin or Hero perspective, as many stories have an element of self-fulfillment and self-sacrifice in them. Alternatively, a writer could weave both aspects into the protagonist, creating a more complex character. A single character could go through the path of a Virgin, fulfilling her dream of developing her talent, and then use that talent to save her community, in true Hero fashion. Also, a screenplay could have two protagonists or a Virgin protagonist and a strong supporting Hero character, for example. Each journey could be well developed with crossover points that are inherent to their archetypal structures. The addition of a second theory for archetypal structure not only enhances the telling of feminine stories. It also provides a structural framework for several combinations in storytelling and sharpens an understanding of each structure.

In the story of Adam and Eve there are two trees with forbidden fruit: the tree of knowledge and the tree of life or immortality. When Eve takes an apple from the tree of knowledge, she becomes aware of her nakedness and sexuality. This is the journey of the Virgin to know herself and bring that knowledge to life. She claims her personal autonomy through the awakening of her creativity, spirituality and sexuality as symbolized by the eating of an apple. Cast out of Eden before they can eat from the tree of life and gain immortality, Adam and Eve are banished from the comforts of paradise to a foreign land and forced to survive on their own. This is the Hero's journey of travelling to a foreign land to become brave, rugged, and skilled and test the boundaries of mortality.

The Virgin and the Hero are so foundational to great storytelling that they both occur in ancient scripts and modern movies. *The Virgin's Promise* has challenged the theory of the monomyth and joins the Hero as a root source to great storytelling. Together the Virgin and the Hero archetypal structures guide writers to reach into the unconscious world and dazzle audiences. This is only the beginning.

Virgin Movie Title:	Protagonist:	Main Characters:

1. Dependent World

2. Price of Conformity

3. Opportunity to Shine

4. Dresses the Part

5. Secret World

6. No Longer Fits Her World

7. Caught Shining

8. Gives Up What Kept Her Stuck

9. Kingdom in Chaos

10. Wanders in the Wilderness

11. Chooses Her Light

12. Re-Ordering (Rescue)

13. The Kingdom Is Brighter

Hero Movie Title:	Protagonist:	Main Characters:

2. Call to Adventure

3. Refusal of the Call

4. Meeting with the Guide

5. Tests, Allies, Enemies

6. Crosses the First Threshold

7. Preparations

8. Crisis

9. Reward

10. Road Back

11. Final Battle

12. Return with the Elixir

Working Title:

Central Question
(Price of Conformity & Opportunity to Shine – Virgin;
Refusal of the Call and Call to Adventure – Hero)

Inciting Incident
(Opportunity to Shine – Virgin; Call to Adventure – Hero)

Moment of Doubt
(Wanders in the Wilderness – Virgin; Crisis – Hero)

Act III Climax
(Chooses Her Light & Reordering – Virgin; Final Battle – Hero)

Appendix 3

Character Symbolism Worksheet

| | Feminine Archetypes | | Masculine Archetypes | |
	light	*shadow*	*light*	*shadow*
beginning	virgin, princess, prince, maiden, artist, rebel, child	whore, victim, slave, prostitute, sad clown	hero, heroine, adventurer, liberator, rescuer, avenger, savior, cowboy	coward, bully, eternal child
middle	mother, father, goddess, god, healer, storyteller, priestess, priest, Samaritan	femme fatale, vampire, wicked stepmother, bitch/ manipulator	lover, king, queen, warrior, mediator, judge, angel, advocate	tyrant, evil queen, dictator, destroyer
end	crone, fairy godmother, trickster, fool, jester, shape – shifter, mystic, alchemist	hag, lecher, thief, saboteur, cougar, gossip, Don Juan	mentor, wise man, wise woman, philanthropist, benefactor	miser, spinster, hermit

Film List

About a Boy* – 32, 36, 61, 68, 73, 77, 78

Alien* – 14, 116, 117, 121, 124, 127, 129

Aladdin – 39

Angels in the Outfield* – 22, 31, 44, 79, 164

Antonia's Line – 13

Away From Her – 16

The Banger Sisters – 167

Beauty and the Beast – 8, 11, 16

Bend It Like Beckham* – 10, 22, 30, 38, 52, 54, 63, 65, 69, 80, 156

Better Than Chocolate – xxiv

Beverly Hills Cop* – 108, 119, 120, 123, 125, 127, 130, 148, 158, 161, 162

Billy Elliot* – 10, 18, 21, 31, 37, 42, 45, 47, 56, 57, 65, 67, 68, 77, 82, 156, 160, 164

Blood Diamond* – 108, 109, 112, 115, 117, 118, 123, 124, 125, 128, 131, 148, 158

Bollywood/Hollywood* – 21, 30, 33, 40, 49, 65, 67, 72, 82, 83

The Bourne Identity* – 117, 118, 123, 133, 150

The Bridges of Madison County – 14

Bridget Jones's Diary – 53

Brokeback Mountain* – xxiv, 21, 48, 49, 51, 53, 57, 58, 63, 68, 71.83, 156

Camelot – 4

Casino Royale – 14

The Children's Hour – xxiv

Chocolat – 13

A Christmas Carol – 17

Cinderella – 35, 39

Clueless – 32, 36

Dangerous Liaisons – 17

Dark Knight – 4

Dirty Dancing – 35, 71

Do You Remember Dolly Bell? – 51

Ella Enchanted – 53

Enchanted April – 13

Erin Brockovich* – 22, 84, 152, 156

Ever After* – xxiii, 3, 20, 27, 34, 35, 39, 40, 45, 47, 51, 53, 56,

57, 59, 63, 68, 70, 73, 75, 86, 153, 156

The Firm* – 108, 110, 113, 115, 118, 119, 124, 127, 134, 158

Fried Green Tomatoes – 16

The 40 Year Old Virgin – 101, 102, 103, 104

The Full Monty – 34

The Godfather – 15

The Graduate – 16

Happy Feet – 153

Heavenly Creatures – 41

The Insider – 115

The Last Samurai – 124

Legally Blond* – 32, 37, 44, 48, 56, 77, 87, 88, 105, 148, 156, 164

Legends of the Fall – 112

Liar Liar – 17

Little Miss Sunshine – 164

Lord of the Rings – 27, 108

Maid in Manhattan* – 27, 38, 45, 49, 59, 65, 68, 76, 88, 153, 156

Mamma Mia! – 101, 102, 103, 105

The Matrix* – 10, 12, 27, 107, 109, 114, 123, 125, 136, 137, 169

Me and the Prince – 53

Michael Clayton – 14

Miss Congeniality* – 46, 47, 56, 61, 89

Mrs. Doubtfire – 13

Mulan – xxiii, 30, 44, 120, 152

New Waterford Girl* – 32, 40, 52, 55, 65, 73, 90

An Officer and a Gentleman – 115, 124

101 Dalmatians – 176

The Other Boleyn Girl – 11, 33

Pocahontas – 32

Pretty Woman* – 32, 35, 36, 40, 46, 47, 48, 49, 52, 55, 61, 67, 68, 72, 73, 91, 157, 163

Pride & Prejudice – 33

The Princess Bride* – 108, 119, 137

Princess Diaries – 46, 47

Private Benjamin – 115

Raiders of the Lost Arc – 124

The Reader – 16

Rocky – xxiv, 22

Roman Holiday – 35

Romancing the Stone* – 117, 119, 121, 127, 129, 138

Shakespeare in Love* – 10, 22, 27, 34, 42, 43, 52, 53, 54, 55, 59, 69, 92

Shrek – xxiii, 63

Sister Act* – 35, 39, 55, 65, 66, 71, 76, 93

Sleeping Beauty – 36, 39

Snow White – 34, 35, 176

Some Like It Hot – 117

The Sound of Music* – 40, 58, 155

Star Wars – 10, 27, 110, 116, 117, 122, 127, 163

Stealing Beauty – 51

Strictly Ballroom* – xxiv, 22, 38, 46, 47, 52, 59, 62, 69, 76, 95, 148, 158

The Terminal – 14

Thelma and Louise – 111, 128

Thirteen – 17

Top Gun – 112

Tootsie – 58

Unforgiven* – 25, 108, 111, 113, 117, 122, 126, 140, 158

The Virgin Suicides* – 41, 62, 96

Wedding Crashers* – xxiv, 35, 45, 53, 55, 69

The Wedding Singer – 164

Whale Rider – 33

What a Girl Wants – 34, 75

While You Were Sleeping* – 30, 36, 42, 53, 54, 56, 58, 65, 77, 98, 153

Willow* – 21, 27, 35, 108, 110, 116, 120, 129

Witness – 128

The Wizard of Oz – 27, 115, 123

Women: A True Story: 2, The Power Game – 26

Women on the Verge of a Nervous Breakdown – 13

Working Girl* – 27, 42, 43, 49, 52, 58, 61, 66, 70, 73, 76, 99, 153, 164

---

*See Film Summary

Selected References

Bettelheim, Bruno. *The Uses of Enchantment: The Meaning and Importance of Fairy Tales.* New York: Vintage Books, 1989 (1975).

Campbell, Joseph. *The Hero with a Thousand Faces.* Second edition. Princeton, New Jersey: Bollingen Series/Princeton University Press, 1973 (1968).

Fields, Syd. *Screenplay: The Foundation of Screenwriting.* Fourth edition. New York: Dell Publishing, 2005.

Hauge, Michael. *Writing Screenplays That Sell.* New York: HarperCollins, 1991 (1988).

Hollis, James. *Mythogems: Incarnations of the Invisible World.* Toronto: Inner City Books, 2004.

——. *Tracking the Gods: The Place of Myth in Modern Life.* Toronto: Inner City Books, 1995.

Johnson, Robert A. *Femininity Lost and Regained.* New York: Harper and Row, 1990.

Jung, Carl. *Memories, Dreams, Reflections.* Edited by Aniela Jaffe. Translated by Richard and Clara Winston. New York: Vintage Books, 1965.

——. *The Portable Jung.* Introduction by Joseph Campbell. Translated by R.F.C. Hull. New York: Penguin Books, 1976.

King, Viki. *How to Write a Movie in 21 Days.* New York: HarperCollins, 1988.

McKee, Robert. *Story.* New York: HarperCollins, 1997.

Moore, Robert L., and Douglas Gillette. *King, Warrior, Magician, Lover: Rediscovering the Archetypes of Mature Masculinity.* New York: HarperCollins, 1990.

Murdock, Maureen. *The Hero's Daughter.* Toronto: Ballantine Books, 1994.

Ong, Walter. *Orality and Literacy: The Technologizing of the World.* New York: Routledge, 1991 (1982).

Schenk, Ronald. *The Soul of Beauty: a Psychological Investigation of Appearance.* Lewisburg, Pennsylvania: Bucknell University Press, 1994 (1992).

Snyder, Blake. *Save the Cat: The Last Book on Screenwriting You'll Ever Need.* Studio City, California: Michael Wiese Productions, 2005.

Stein, Murray. *Jung's Map of the World: An Introduction.* Peru, Illinois: Open Court Publishing Company, 2005 (1998).

Tuan, Yi-Fu. *Passing Strange and Wonderful: Aesthetics, Nature and Culture.* Washington, D.C.: Island Press, 1993.

Turner, Victor. *The Ritual Process.* Ithaca, New York: Cornell University Press, 1969.

Ulanov, Ann, and Barry Ulanov. *Cinderella and her Sisters: The Envied and the Envying.* Third edition. Einsiedeln, Switzerland: Daimon Verlag, 2007.

Vogler, Christopher. *The Writer's Journey: Mythic Structures for Writers.* Second edition. Studio City, California: Michael Wiese Productions, 1998.

Walliman, Isodor. "On Max Weber's Definition of Power." *Australia New Zealand Journal of Sociology,* Vol. 13, No. 3 (1977), 231-235.

Wolf, Naomi. *The Beauty Myth.* Toronto: Vintage Books, 1991.

Woodman, Marion. *The Pregnant Virgin: A Process of Psychological Transformation.* Toronto: Inner City Books, 1985.

Zipes, Jack. *Fairy Tale as Myth – Myth as Fairy Tale.* Lexington, Kentucky: University Press of Kentucky, 1994.

About the Author

Kim Hudson grew up in the Yukon, a father's daughter with a Cinderella complex. She spent many years exploring her masculine side as a field geologist and a First Nations Land Claims negotiator before studying at Vancouver Film School, University of British Columbia, and the International School of Analytical Psychology Zurich. Kim's personal journey and scholarly inquiry combined to develop this theory of the Virgin's archetypal structure. Over the past four years Kim has given courses and workshops on the Virgin's Promise in the Vancouver area.

For information about Kim's seminars and workshops or consultation on the archetypal structure of a screenplay, novel or concept please contact kimh@vfs.com or visit kehudson.wordpress.com

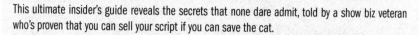

SELLING YOUR STORY IN 60 SECONDS

THE GUARANTEED WAY TO GET YOUR SCREENPLAY OR NOVEL READ

MICHAEL HAUGE

Best-selling author Michael Hauge reveals:

- How to Design, Practice and Present the 60-Second Pitch
- The Cardinal Rule of Pitching
- The 10 Key Components of a Commercial Story
- The 8 Steps to a Powerful Pitch
- Targeting Your Buyers
- Securing Opportunities to Pitch
- Pitching Templates
- And much more, including "The Best Pitch I Ever Heard," an exclusive collection from major film executives

"Michael Hauge's principles and methods are so well argued that the mysteries of effective screenwriting can be understood — even by directors."
> – Phillip Noyce, Director, *Patriot Games, Clear and Present Danger, The Quiet American, Rabbit Proof Fence*

"... one of the few authentically good teachers out there. Every time I revisit my notes, I learn something new or reinforce something that I need to remember."
> – Jeff Arch, Screenwriter, *Sleepless in Seattle, Iron Will*

"Michael Hauge's method is magic — but unlike most magicians, he shows you how the trick is done."
> – William Link, Screenwriter & Co-Creator, *Columbo; Murder, She Wrote*

"By following the formula we learned in Michael Hauge's seminar, we got an agent, optioned our script, and now have a three picture deal at Disney."
> – Paul Hoppe and David Henry, Screenwriters

MICHAEL HAUGE, is the author of *Writing Screenplays That Sell*, now in its 30th printing, and has presented his seminars and lectures to more than 30,000 writers and filmmakers. He has coached hundreds of screenwriters and producers on their screenplays and pitches, and has consulted on projects for Warner Brothers, Disney, New Line, CBS, Lifetime, Julia Roberts, Jennifer Lopez, Kirsten Dunst, and Morgan Freeman.

$12.95 · 150 PAGES · ORDER NUMBER 64RLS · ISBN: 1932907203

CINEMATIC STORYTELLING

THE 100 MOST POWERFUL FILM CONVENTIONS EVERY FILMMAKER MUST KNOW

JENNIFER VAN SIJLL

BEST SELLER

How do directors use screen direction to suggest conflict? How do screenwriters exploit film space to show change? How does editing style determine emotional response?

Many first-time writers and directors do not ask these questions. They forego the huge creative resource of the film medium, defaulting to dialog to tell their screen story. Yet most movies are carried by sound and picture. The industry's most successful writers and directors have mastered the cinematic conventions specific to the medium. They have harnessed non-dialog techniques to create some of the most cinematic moments in movie history.

This book is intended to help writers and directors more fully exploit the medium's inherent storytelling devices. It contains 100 non-dialog techniques that have been used by the industry's top writers and directors. From *Metropolis* and *Citizen Kane* to *Dead Man* and *Kill Bill*, the book illustrates — through 500 frame grabs and 75 script excerpts — how the inherent storytelling devices specific to film were exploited.

You will learn:
- How non-dialog film techniques can advance story.
- How master screenwriters exploit cinematic conventions to create powerful scenarios.

"Cinematic Storytelling scores a direct hit in terms of concise information and perfectly chosen visuals, and it also searches out... and finds... an emotional core that many books of this nature either miss or are afraid of."
— Kirsten Sheridan, Director, *Disco Pigs*; Co-writer, *In America*

"Here is a uniquely fresh, accessible, and truly original contribution to the field. Jennifer van Sijll takes her readers in a wholly new direction, integrating aspects of screenwriting with all the film crafts in a way I've never before seen. It is essential reading not only for screenwriters but also for filmmakers of every stripe."
— Prof. Richard Walter, UCLA Screenwriting Chairman

JENNIFER VAN SIJLL has taught film production, film history, and screenwriting. She is currently on the faculty at San Francisco State's Department of Cinema.

$24.95 · 230 PAGES · ORDER # 35RLS · ISBN: 193290705X

24 HOURS | 1.800.833.5738 | WWW.MWP.COM

THE MYTH OF MWP

In a dark time, a light bringer came along, leading the curious and the frustrated to clarity and empowerment. It took the well-guarded secrets out of the hands of the few and made them available to all. It spread a spirit of openness and creative freedom, and built a storehouse of knowledge dedicated to the betterment of the arts.

The essence of the Michael Wiese Productions (MWP) is empowering people who have the burning desire to express themselves creatively. We help them realize their dreams by putting the tools in their hands. We demystify the sometimes secretive worlds of screenwriting, directing, acting, producing, film financing, and other media crafts.

By doing so, we hope to bring forth a realization of 'conscious media' which we define as being positively charged, emphasizing hope and affirming positive values like trust, cooperation, self-empowerment, freedom, and love. Grounded in the deep roots of myth, it aims to be healing both for those who make the art and those who encounter it. It hopes to be transformative for people, opening doors to new possibilities and pulling back veils to reveal hidden worlds.

MWP has built a storehouse of knowledge unequaled in the world, for no other publisher has so many titles on the media arts. Please visit www.mwp.com where you will find many free resources and a 25% discount on our books. Sign up and become part of the wider creative community!

Onward and upward,

Michael Wiese
Publisher/Filmmaker

FILM & VIDEO BOOKS

TO RECEIVE A FREE MWP NEWSLETTER, CLICK ON WWW.MWP.COM TO REGISTER

SCREENWRITING | WRITING

And the Best Screenplay Goes to... | Dr. Linda Seger | $26.95
Archetypes for Writers | Jennifer Van Bergen | $22.95
Ball Brothers | Lacy Waltzman, Matthew Bishop, Michael Wiese | $12.95
Cinematic Storytelling | Jennifer Van Sijll | $24.95
Could It Be a Movie? | Christina Hamlett | $26.95
Creating Characters | Marisa D'Vari | $26.95
Crime Writer's Reference Guide, The | Martin Roth | $20.95
Deep Cinema | Mary Trainor-Brigham | $19.95
Elephant Bucks | Sheldon Bull | $24.95
Fast, Cheap & Written That Way | John Gaspard | $26.95
Hollywood Standard – 2nd Edition, The | Christopher Riley | $18.95
Horror Screenwriting | Devin Watson | $24.95
I Could've Written a Better Movie than That! | Derek Rydall | $26.95
Inner Drives | Pamela Jaye Smith | $26.95
Moral Premise, The | Stanley D. Williams, Ph.D. | $24.95
Myth and the Movies | Stuart Voytilla | $26.95
Power of the Dark Side, The | Pamela Jaye Smith | $22.95
Psychology for Screenwriters | William Indick, Ph.D. | $26.95
Reflections of the Shadow | Jeffrey Hirschberg | $26.95
Rewrite | Paul Chitlik | $16.95
Romancing the A-List | Christopher Keane | $18.95
Save the Cat! | Blake Snyder | $19.95
Save the Cat! Goes to the Movies | Blake Snyder | $24.95
Screenwriting 101 | Neill D. Hicks | $16.95
Screenwriting for Teens | Christina Hamlett | $18.95
Script-Selling Game, The | Kathie Fong Yoneda | $16.95
Stealing Fire From the Gods, 2nd Edition | James Bonnet | $26.95
Talk the Talk | Penny Penniston | $24.95
Way of Story, The | Catherine Ann Jones | $22.95
What Are You Laughing At? | Brad Schreiber | $19.95
Writer's Journey – 3rd Edition, The | Christopher Vogler | $26.95
Writer's Partner, The | Martin Roth | $24.95
Writing the Action Adventure Film | Neill D. Hicks | $14.95
Writing the Comedy Film | Stuart Voytilla & Scott Petri | $14.95
Writing the Killer Treatment | Michael Halperin | $14.95
Writing the Second Act | Michael Halperin | $19.95
Writing the Thriller Film | Neill D. Hicks | $14.95
Writing the TV Drama Series, 2nd Edition | Pamela Douglas | $26.95
Your Screenplay Sucks! | William M. Akers | $19.95

FILMMAKING

Film School | Richard D. Pepperman | $24.95
Power of Film, The | Howard Suber | $27.95

PITCHING

Perfect Pitch – 2nd Edition, The | Ken Rotcop | $19.95
Selling Your Story in 60 Seconds | Michael Hauge | $12.95

SHORTS

Filmmaking for Teens, 2nd Edition | Troy Lanier & Clay Nichols | $24.95
Making It Big in Shorts | Kim Adelman | $22.95

BUDGET | PRODUCTION MANAGEMENT

Film & Video Budgets, 5th Updated Edition | Deke Simon | $26.95
Film Production Management 101 | Deborah S. Patz | $39.95

DIRECTING | VISUALIZATION

Animation Unleashed | Ellen Besen | $26.95

Cinematography for Directors | Jacqueline Frost | $29.95
Citizen Kane Crash Course in Cinematography | David Worth | $19.95
Directing Actors | Judith Weston | $26.95
Directing Feature Films | Mark Travis | $26.95
Fast, Cheap & Under Control | John Gaspard | $26.95
Film Directing: Cinematic Motion, 2nd Edition | Steven D. Katz | $27.95
Film Directing: Shot by Shot | Steven D. Katz | $27.95
Film Director's Intuition, The | Judith Weston | $26.95
First Time Director | Gil Bettman | $27.95
From Word to Image, 2nd Edition | Marcie Begleiter | $26.95
I'll Be in My Trailer! | John Badham & Craig Modderno | $26.95
Master Shots | Christopher Kenworthy | $24.95
Setting Up Your Scenes | Richard D. Pepperman | $24.95
Setting Up Your Shots, 2nd Edition | Jeremy Vineyard | $22.95
Working Director, The | Charles Wilkinson | $22.95

DIGITAL | DOCUMENTARY | SPECIAL

Digital Filmmaking 101, 2nd Edition | Dale Newton & John Gaspard | $26.95
Digital Moviemaking 3.0 | Scott Billups | $24.95
Digital Video Secrets | Tony Levelle | $26.95
Greenscreen Made Easy | Jeremy Hanke & Michele Yamazaki | $19.95
Producing with Passion | Dorothy Fadiman & Tony Levelle | $22.95
Special Effects | Michael Slone | $31.95

EDITING

Cut by Cut | Gael Chandler | $35.95
Cut to the Chase | Bobbie O'Steen | $24.95
Eye is Quicker, The | Richard D. Pepperman | $27.95
Film Editing | Gael Chandler | $34.95
Invisible Cut, The | Bobbie O'Steen | $28.95

SOUND | DVD | CAREER

Complete DVD Book, The | Chris Gore & Paul J. Salamoff | $26.95
Costume Design 101, 2nd Edition | Richard La Motte | $24.95
Hitting Your Mark, 2nd Edition | Steve Carlson | $22.95
Sound Design | David Sonnenschein | $19.95
Sound Effects Bible, The | Ric Viers | $26.95
Storyboarding 101 | James Fraioli | $19.95
There's No Business Like Soul Business | Derek Rydall | $22.95
You Can Act! | D.W. Brown | $24.95

FINANCE | MARKETING | FUNDING

Art of Film Funding, The | Carole Lee Dean | $26.95
Bankroll | Tom Malloy | $26.95
Complete Independent Movie Marketing Handbook, The | Mark Steven Bosko | $39.95
Getting the Money | Jeremy Jusso | $26.95
Independent Film and Videomakers Guide – 2nd Edition, The | Michael Wiese | $29.95
Independent Film Distribution | Phil Hall | $26.95
Shaking the Money Tree, 3rd Edition | Morrie Warshawski | $26.95

MEDITATION | ART

Mandalas of Bali | Dewa Nyoman Batuan | $39.95

OUR FILMS

Dolphin Adventures: DVD | Michael Wiese and Hardy Jones | $24.95
Hardware Wars: DVD | Written and Directed by Ernie Fosselius | $14.95
On the Edge of a Dream | Michael Wiese | $16.95
Sacred Sites of the Dalai Lamas– DVD, The | Documentary by Michael Wiese | $24.95

CPSIA information can be obtained
at www.ICGtesting.com
Printed in the USA
BVHW041626030719
552582BV00017B/926/P